THE 100 one hundred greatest MOMENTS AT THE Olympics

The one hundred greatest MOMENTS AT THE Olympics

WRITTEN BY

MARK CROSSLAND WITH **MIKE WOOD**

WITH A FOREWORD BY

DALEY THOMPSON

generation
PUBLICATIONS

"To Jack Crossland and Dennis Morse"

Designed by Robert Kelland

GENERATION PUBLICATIONS

Editor: Phil McNeill
Publications Manager: Eve Cossins
Publishers: David Crowe and Mark Peacock

With thanks to Adrian Waddington;
and to Lara Piercy and Rob Brown at Colour Systems

Special thanks to Daley Thompson

First published in Great Britain in 2000 by Generation Publications
9 Holyrood Street, London SE1 2EL
020 7403 0364
genpub@btinternet.com

Text copyright © Generation Publications 2000

ISBN 1 903009 37 5

Production by Mike Powell & Associates (01494 676891)
Origination by Colour Systems Ltd, London
Printed in Slovenia by arrangement with Korotan-Ljubljana d.o.o.

The photographs in the book are from Allsport, with thanks to Rob Harborne and Matt Stevens,
and Phil Burnham-Richards at Hulton Getty;
and from Corbis, with thanks to Helen Dobson

Page 1: The Olympic flag
Page 2: Gail Devers at Atlanta, 1996
Page 3: Michael Johnson at Atlanta, 1996

Mark Crossland has done the research and statistics for numerous sport books, including eight others in the *100 Greatest* series. He grew up in West Yorkshire, where his love for sport was honed at Elland Road, Headingley and Belle Vue – home to Wakefield Trinity.

Mike Wood has been a contributor to *Golf Monthly* magazine for six years and has written several books on sporting topics. His latest is *Five Go To War* – a history of the Five Nations rugby championship. A one-time prop forward, he now lives in the Olympic city of Sydney.

Contents

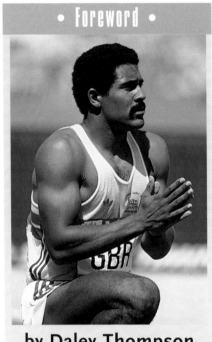

• Foreword •

by Daley Thompson

The Olympics isn't only the greatest show on earth – for those who compete, it is also the ultimate test. This is what it's all about.

To enter is a privilege. To win a medal is a dream.

To win the gold ... well, it was certainly one of the highlights of my life.

In this book you'll find the stories of many great athletes who have achieved the highest pinnacle in their sport: Carl Lewis with his amazing nine gold medals; the iron man Steve Redgrave with his four golds in a row; Steffi Graf's golden slam; Seb Coe, Steve Ovett, Wilma Rudolph, Olga Korbut – all the usual suspects.

But the Olympic ideal isn't just about winning. It's also about striving to do your best, being honest to yourself. Like Dorando Pietri, the Italian marathon man who collapsed over the line at White City in 1908 and then was disqualified because the stewards had helped him over. (Mind you, they'd have to give me a medal just for entering the marathon...) The Olympics is also about taking a stand. Against cheats such as Ben Johnson, whose story appears here as the darker side of the Olympic coin. Or against prejudice – an ideal embodied by Jesse Owens in 1936, when he showed Hitler that all races are equal.

Looking forward to the Sydney Olympics and beyond, it won't be easy for sport to rid itself of the drug-takers, though it's a battle we have to win if the Games are to survive as a true test of athletic ability. But I am confident that the Olympic Games will continue to bring people together from around the world – athletes competing in friendship and respect, living alongside one another in the Village, and showing the world a better way to express national pride.

We all have our favourite moments at the Olympics. I'm sure you'll find yours somewhere in these pages. And if you're a youngster with the ambition to be an athlete, judo player, horse rider or boxer ... who knows, in some future edition of *The 100 Greatest Moments At The Olympics*, it may even be you writing this foreword!

Moments to remember: The sheer determination of Marathon runner Dorando Pietri nearing the stadium in 1908; the grace of Olga Korbut in 1972; the triumph of Carl Lewis after leaping to golden glory in 1996; and Pinsent and Redgrave rowing into the record books, also in 1996

Introduction

by Mark Crossland

Great Olympic moments are not necessarily only the winning ones. For example, how many can name the winner of the ski-jump at the 1988 Calgary Winter Olympics? Very few. Yet millions remember the efforts of Eddie 'The Eagle' Edwards, who came last in the same event. Colonel Harry Llewellyn's heroics in obtaining Britain's only gold medal at the 1952 Helsinki Games would probably be seen as a great moment only by the British public. But some moments stand out as being great to observers around the globe. The feats of Jesse Owens at Berlin in 1936, for example.

So for this book, I have chosen moments from a range of sports to go beside those that choose themselves. I have not forgotten the exploits of the early Olympians. Indeed, it is these athletes who sum up the true spirit of the Olympics. Athletes who travelled halfway round the world in the days before jets made it quick and easy. Athletes who, when the Games were a truly amateur event, made great financial sacrifices so that they could take part and test themselves against the best that other countries had to offer. And athletes who simply wanted to be there and compete even though they had little chance of success.

These competitors have been as important as the great champions in helping to shape the Games and turn them into the global spectacular that we enjoy today, and you'll find them represented here as well.

Top row, left to right: Spyridon Louis, Dorando Pietri, Paavo Nurmi, Amsterdam 1928 poster, Jackie Joyner-Kersee.
Middle row, left to right: Nadia Comaneci, Daley Thompson, fireworks at Sydney, Jesse Owens, Paris 1924 poster.
Bottom row, left to right: Seb Coe, Eric Liddell, diving at Atlanta, Andrey Chemerkin, Marie-Jose Perec.
Opposite: The opening ceremony at Atlanta, 1996

Milo *factfile*

Born: c. 552 BC, Kroton, Southern Italy
Country: Italy
Olympic record:

540 BC: won boys' wrestling
532 BC: wrestling champion
528 BC: wrestling champion
524 BC: wrestling champion
520 BC: wrestling champion
516 BC: wrestling champion
512 BC: wrestling runner-up

Greek wrestlers from a 510 BC sculpture

1

The real Hercules
Olympia 540 - 512 BC

"It is no great thing to possess strength, whatever kind it is, but to use it as one should. For of what advantage to Milo of Kroton was his enormous strength of body?"
Diodorus Siculus, Historical Library

The Olympic Games were born in the shadow of Mount Olympus, home of the Greek gods, centuries before the birth of Christ. City states from around the world sent athletes to compete. With the roads to the venue lined with great statues of Zeus and the stadium filled with artists, poets and great leaders, the ancient Olympic Games were a celebration of Greek life.

The modern Olympics, with vast marketing machines and growing professionalism, may seem a far cry from the Games of antiquity. A closer inspection, however, shows a different story. The ancient Games were often a vehicle for political ambitions and personal glory where the stakes were high. This inevitably brought about heroes and villains alike. In fact, the statues of Zeus were built with the money from fines handed out to people found cheating. As for the stars in those days, the biggest, in more ways than one, was Milo of Kroton.

His immense strength has been well documented. According to one story, a building collapsed during a meeting to celebrate the philosopher Pythagoras, and Milo literally held up the roof so his fellow Pythagoreans were able to flee the place safely, before dashing to safety himself.

His greatest achievement, however, is one that has never been bettered in the modern Games – the winning of five consecutive Olympic crowns. These great victories took place during the period of 532 to 516 BC in the wrestling event, where Milo's natural power was enough to beat all-comers.

He eventually succumbed to defeat in his sixth Olympiad. Refusing to retire, he competed in the 67th Olympiad in 512 BC despite being well over 40 years old. His much younger opponent in the final won the contest not by overpowering Milo, but by avoiding the older wrestler and eventually wearing him out.

First blood to USA
Athens 1896

When Frenchman Pierre de Coubertin proposed an Olympic Games to coincide with the World Fair of 1900 in Paris, the international community was so enthusiastic that it was decided to hold one earlier. The venue for these Games was never in doubt – Greece, home of the ancient Olympics. So on April 6, 1896, King George I of Greece opened the first modern Olympic Games in a new purpose-built stadium in Athens.

Two hundred athletes, all men, took part from 14 countries from as far afield as the USA and Australia. The Americans sent over a very strong athletics team and won nine of the 12 track and field events, thus starting a tradition of success throughout the Olympics.

It was therefore no surprise that the first winner of an Olympic competition was an American. James Brendan Connolly, a member of the City of Suffolk Athletic Club, hopped, skipped and jumped his way into the history books with a leap of 13.71 metres in the triple jump to take first place a full one metre ahead of Frenchman Alexandre Tuffère. Connolly was a deserving winner, having made considerable sacrifices to compete in the Games. A student at Harvard, he was refused leave and duly dropped out of school. He also had to fully finance his own trip to Europe. Years later, the Ivy League college gave Connolly an honorary degree to mark his efforts.

He did not, however, receive an Olympic medal. Winners of the first modern Games received a certificate, an olive branch and a silver medal. Runners-up had a laurel sprig and a copper medal.

> *"May it be, oh King, that the revival of Olympic games binds closer the links of mutual affection of the Greek and of other peoples."*
>
> The Crown Prince of Greece at the opening ceremony

Connolly *factfile*

Born: 1868, USA **Died:** 1957
Country: USA
Olympic record: 1896: triple jump gold, high jump silver, long jump bronze. 1900: triple jump silver

Proud: Medal winner James Connolly

Above: An 1896 engraving of Edwin Flack. The drawing, right, shows Spyridon Louis (1873-1940), winning the 40 km marathon at the first modern Olympic Games held in Athens in 1896. He was later chosen to kindle the Olympic flame at the 1936 Berlin Olympics

It's Flack's track
Athens 1896

With nine of the twelve track and field events going the way of America in the inaugural Games, the remaining three were shared between two countries. Spyridon Louis took the marathon gold for the host country amid a wave of great nationalistic pride. The true star of the track, however, was Australian middle-distance runner Eddie Flack who was the only man representing his country.

His effort was exhaustive, to say the least, as he had to run four races in five days. He began with the 800 metres trials, winning his heat to ensure a place in the final. The following day he took part in the final of the 1500 metres, where he gained the first of his two victories in a closely contested race, finishing less than a second ahead of the Hungarian Nandor Dani.

After a day of rest, Flack entered the 800 metres final. Again he won a close race, finishing just ahead of Arthur Black of the USA.

Not content with such a powerful performance, the Australian chose to enter the marathon on the fifth day. After making a solo break from the pack, things were looking good until, with just four kilometres remaining, his exploits finally caught up with him and he was overtaken by Spyridon Louis, the eventual winner.

Though he failed to finish the race, Flack's overall performance at the Games was such that he would return home to a hero's welcome.

Game, set and gold

Paris 1900

The 1900 Olympic Games in Paris were contested in conjunction with the World Fair of that year and the Games were spread over five months. The top-class organisation that such a long haul needed was lacking and the Games were less successful than those in Athens four years earlier. There were plus points, however. For a start, more than a thousand athletes from 26 countries lined up. And women took part in the Olympics for the first time.

With mixed feelings, the world awaited the crowning of the first female Olympic champion. The honour went to British tennis player Charlotte Cooper, though her victory in the singles final came as no real surprise.

Charlotte had won the Wimbledon championship on three occasions, the last in 1898. It meant she was a favourite to take the Olympic tennis crown. Her victory in the final against French girl Helene Prevost was followed by another triumph in the mixed doubles. Pairing with countryman Reginald Doherty in the final, she again beat the unlucky Prevost who had teamed with Irishman Harold Mahony.

Charlotte Cooper went on to win a further two Wimbledon titles but it will be as the first female Olympic champion that she will be remembered.

British tennis ace Charlotte Cooper was the world's first female Olympic champion

Marathon pick-me-up

St Louis 1904

the dominance of US athletes taking part. Of 687 competitors, more than 500 were from the host country who, not surprisingly, won a total of 238 medals.

One event that did capture the imagination, perhaps for bizarre reasons, was the marathon. Run in a sweltering 90 degrees, the race was understandably slow, the first man home – American Fred Lorz – coming in at 3 hours 28 minutes and 35 seconds. He was not, however, to be the winner. It was later discovered that Lorz, who celebrated his victory in the sapping race with a remarkable display of energetic euphoria, had hitched a lift in a lorry to the stadium precincts. He was disqualified and banned for life.

English-born American Thomas Hicks was proclaimed the victor but it transpired his run was painful to say the least and worthy of the exhortation, 'Don't try this at home, kids'. Along the punishing route he was regularly fed a mixture of brandy and strychnine to keep him going! As unorthodox and dangerous as it sounds, it worked.

Above: Proud Thomas Hicks with his trophies

Like the previous Games, the 1904 Olympics, held in America's Deep South, were run in conjunction with a World Fair. And like the Parisian Games, they were a disappointment.

The competition ran over a number of weeks and failed, in general, to catch the imagination of the American public despite

Dorando's staggering victory

London 1908

One of the most enduring images of this or any other modern Olympic Games is of the Italian marathon runner Dorando Pietri being helped over the line at the White City stadium in July 1908. The Games were supposed to have been held in Rome but after the eruption of Mount Vesuvius in 1906 the Italian authorities couldn't cope with the cost of staging the competition. London offered its services.

There was, however, one catch. English pride, some may call it arrogance, meant that they insisted on organising the Games from top to bottom.

Although the event was indeed very well organised, many people, particularly the American contingent, felt that the British competitors were given preferential treatment by the host nation's judges, resulting in Britain's unprecedented gold medal count of 56. After that, all future Olympic Games would use judges from various countries.

Ironically, the American marathon runner John Joseph Hayes had the British judges to thank for his controversial victory.

Teamwork: Dorando Pietri of Italy, on the verge of collapse, is helped across the finishing line by officials in the Marathon of the 1908 Olympics in London

With the Italian Pietri entering the stadium way ahead of the chasing pack, the race looked won. The 100,000 spectators who packed the stadium offered warm applause as Pietri embarked on the final lap. With the finishing line in sight, however, the Italian's legs buckled and he fell to the cinder track. Bravely picking himself up, he unsteadily entered the final straight before falling again. But with glory in sight, the exhausted runner once again managed a vertical stance.

After falling twice more and staggering around like a punch-drunk boxer, many of the judges (some say Arthur Conan Doyle amongst them) moved in to help. They escorted the almost unconscious Pietri across the line to the vociferous cheers of the British public who presumed the result would stand.

Unfortunately, Pietri was later disqualified for having "used external support" and Hayes was declared the winner with a time of 2 hours 55 minutes and 18 seconds. Pietri's efforts were not all in vain, however. The following day Queen Alexandra presented him with a gold trophy she herself donated in acknowledgement of his heroic performance.

The flying Finn
Stockholm 1912

The fifth modern Olympic Games were held in Stockholm and were the first to have representatives from every continent. A total of 2,547 athletes took part from 28 countries. Two marvellous innovations made their debut – the electronic timer was introduced to back up the traditional stopwatch, and track and field events now had the advantage of the photo-finish.

But these Games would best be remembered as the start of Finland's domination of long-distance running events, pioneered by Johannes Petteri ('Hannes') Kolehmainen. In his first final, the 10,000 metres, he dominated the race and finished almost a lap ahead of the American Louis Tewanima. The real excitement, however, was to follow two days later in the 5,000 metres final. Here, Kolehmainen was pitted against the great French runner Jean Bouin, who was the world record holder over 10,000

Johannes Kolehmainen (left) about to pass Jean Bouin to win the 5,000 metres

metres. Bouin had decided to concentrate on the shorter distance, feeling it wasn't possible to win both races in such a short period. The Finnish runner was to prove him wrong after an alarmingly quick race in which the two were inseparable right to the end. Kolehmainen won by less than a metre in 14 minutes 36.6 seconds, which knocked almost half a minute off the world record. He went on to win gold in the cross-country event and silver in the team cross-country race.

Eight years later, he added a marathon gold to his collection but his career was halted by the First World War. His performances in those two Olympics were to inspire a nation as the Finns went on to win 17 of the 21 races between 3,000 and 10,000 metres that were run from 1912 up to the Second World War.

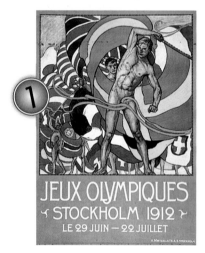

JEUX OLYMPIQUES
⚐ STOCKHOLM 1912 ⚐
LE 29 JUIN – 22 JUILLET

Kolehmainen *factfile*

Born: 9.12.1889, Kuopio
Died: 11.11.1966, Helsinki
Country: Finland
Olympic record: 1912: 5,000 metres gold, 10,000 metres gold, cross-country gold, team cross-country silver
1920: Marathon gold

"I would almost rather not have won than see that flag up there."
Hannes Kolehmainen after the Russian flag was hoisted to celebrate his victories

An Indian summer
Stockholm 1912

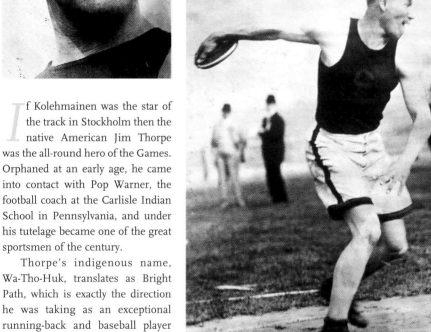

"Sir, you are the greatest athlete in the world."
King Gustav V of Sweden when presenting Thorpe with his medals

If Kolehmainen was the star of the track in Stockholm then the native American Jim Thorpe was the all-round hero of the Games. Orphaned at an early age, he came into contact with Pop Warner, the football coach at the Carlisle Indian School in Pennsylvania, and under his tutelage became one of the great sportsmen of the century.

Thorpe's indigenous name, Wa-Tho-Huk, translates as Bright Path, which is exactly the direction he was taking as an exceptional running-back and baseball player even before his sojourn in Stockholm. He was selected to take part in three events at the Games, the track and field pentathlon, the decathlon and the high-jump. Any mortal might have balked at the size of this task but not Jim Thorpe. He proceeded to thrill the crowds, including the Swedish King, by comprehensively winning the decathlon and pentathlon events. His victory in the decathlon was the most impressive as his points tally was good enough to have won silver in the same event 36 years later.

Thorpe returned to the States as a star and was given a ticker-tape reception in New York. He later proclaimed: "I heard people yelling my name. I couldn't realise how one fellow could have so many friends."

But six months later, it all turned sour when the U.S. Olympic committee declared Thorpe a professional and stripped him of his medals. This didn't halt his success in baseball and American football and in 1950 American sportswriters pronounced him to be the greatest athlete of the first half of the century.

In 1982, the Olympic committee saw the light and posthumously reunited one of the first great Olympians with his gold medals.

Thorpe in Pentathalon action

Thorpe *factfile*

Born: 1887 **Died:** 1953
Country: USA
Olympic record: 1912: Decathlon gold, pentathlon gold, high jump fourth

Old soldier's victory dash
Antwerp 1920

The Olympics resumed in 1920 after a break of eight years as the world indulged in the more pressing matter of the First World War. The choice of Antwerp for the sixth Olympiad was a symbolic gesture as it was on the fields of Belgium that huge sacrifices had been made in the 'war to end all wars'. These Games were to prove that not only sport, but also the world in general had managed to recover from its darkest hour.

Twenty-nine countries took part in Antwerp, one more than had fought in the war, but the standard of competition was depleted as most nations had lost great athletes during the fighting. One man who did come through unscathed after four years' service with the British army was the middle-distance runner Albert Hill. Into his 30s, Hill could have been forgiven for thinking his chance in the Olympics had come too late. And

Hill *factfile*

Born: 1889 **Died:** 1969
Country: England
Olympic record: 1920: 800m gold,
1500m gold, 3,000m team event silver

Albert Hill had come through four years of war and was in his 30s when he ran to double-gold triumph in 1920

with the prospect of five races in five days it seemed his attempt at a double gold in the 800 and 1500 metres was very much an uphill task.

The phlegmatic Englishman took all this in his stride and his unorthodox tactic of sleeping for three hours before each race left him relaxed and refreshed enough to beat all-comers. His victories in the two finals were close affairs, Hill winning in less than a second in both races to become the star of the track. Then he returned to his job as a railway guard.

Charlie is their darling

Chamonix 1924

With the success of sports such as ice-skating and ice-hockey at the Olympics it was only a matter of time before the winter sports had their own Olympic Games. So on 25 January, 1924, 258 men and women from 16 countries gathered in the Alps for the first Winter Olympics in the French town of Chamonix. Dominated by the Scandinavian countries it was, however, an American who wrote his name in the history books by becoming the first winner of a Winter Olympics event.

Charles Jewtraw came from a poor family in Lake Placid, New York, where he learnt how to speed-skate. It was this skill that brought him victory on January 26 in the 500-metre event. His time of 44.0 seconds was just two tenths of a second faster than Oskar Olsen of Norway in second place. The third-place skater was the Finn Clas Thunberg. He went on to win three golds and one silver to add to his bronze in the inaugural event and become the star of the Games.

Charles Jewtraw (right) with Charles Ingraham Gorman of Canada. Jewtraw won the 500 metres speed-skating event in record time

Enter the Chariots of Fire

Paris 1924

In 1924, Paris sought to banish the organisational chaos that beset the Games in the city 24 years earlier. This would be no mean feat with over 3,000 competitors from 44 countries descending on the French capital, but the Games were a great success and celebrated the world over as they became the first to be reported by live radio. This helped to turn the more successful competitors into heroes of film-star status – in some cases, quite literally.

The story of two of the star performers at the Games was turned into a film 57 years later. The Oscar-winning *Chariots of Fire* chronicled the exploits of the two British runners Harold Abrahams and Eric Liddell.

Liddell was a devout Christian who excelled at all sports. He played seven times for Scotland at rugby union, scoring four tries. But it is for his athletic performances, or rather lack of them, that he will be best remembered. As a strongly religious person, he refused to compete on a Sunday. This meant he would miss the 100 metres and 4x100

Chin up: Eric Liddell storms to a world record and victory in the 400m final

Abrahams *factfile*

Born: 1899 **Died:** 1978
Country: England
Olympic record: 1924: 100m gold,
4x100m relay silver

Liddell *factfile*

Born: 1902 **Died:** 1945
Country: Scotland
Olympic record: 1924: 400m gold,
200m bronze

metres relay. But he won the 400 metres with ease and left everyone wondering what might have been had he run in the 100 metres which many felt was his stronger event.

With the Americans dominating the sprints at previous Olympics, it was up to Harold Abrahams to turn the tide in Paris. At 7pm on July 7, he pipped the American Jackson Scholz to the line by just one tenth of a second to win Britain's first gold medal in this event, and along with Eric Liddell etch his name into Olympic and cinematic history.

Weissmuller *factfile*

Born: 2.6.1904, Windber, Pa **Country:** USA
Olympic record: 1924: freestyle 100m gold, freestyle 400m gold, freestyle relay 4x200m gold, water polo bronze. 1928: freestyle 100m gold, freestyle relay 4x200m gold, water polo fifth

Tarzan swings into action
Paris 1924

If Liddell and Abrahams were to have their lives portrayed on screen, then an American just had to go one better. Johnny Weissmuller was just 20 years old when he became the star of the pool in Paris. He picked up three golds in the 100 metres, 400 metres, and 4x200-metre freestyle events and a bronze medal with the water polo team. These feats confirmed him as the world's greatest swimmer and turned him into an all-American hero. All this didn't go unnoticed at the MGM studios.

Four years later, he added another two gold medals to his tally and was training to compete in the 1932 Olympics when the call came from MGM to star in the first Tarzan movie with sound. The transition from sports star to movie star ran smoothly and Weissmuller starred in 11 Tarzan movies, all thanks to his excellent swimming ability.

To this day, it is still debated who is the greatest-ever swimmer, Johnny Weissmuller or Mark Spitz. Many of the races that Spitz won were not Olympic events when Weissmuller competed.

If they were, then we can only imagine how many gold medals Weissmuller would have added to his total in Paris.

Left: Weissmuller at the 1924 Games

Chivalry comes first
Amsterdam 1928

The ninth summer Olympics took place in Amsterdam over three months in 1928. They were the biggest Games so far with over 3,000 competitors and thousands of spectators packing the new Olympic stadium to see such heroes as Paavo Nurmi.

The 'Phantom Finn' was already a great Olympian before he starred in the Dutch Games. In 1920, he had won three gold medals and one silver, and four years later won a further five gold medals. This included arguably his greatest achievement when he took gold in the 5,000 metres just 40 minutes after winning the 1500 metres race.

It was in Amsterdam, however, where he showed his true Olympic spirit. Nurmi was famous not just for his victories but for always running with a stopwatch to pace himself perfectly. In the semi-finals of the steeplechase, he fell at the water jump and dropped his watch into the water. Frenchman Lucien Duquesne stopped to help the Finn to his feet and find his watch. Nurmi ran the

13

Right: Paavo Nurmi (right) and Lucien Duquesne reach the finish of the 3,000 metres steeplechase semi-final at the Amsterdam Olympics. The Finn offered first place to the Frenchman, who had helped him up after he fell in the race

Nurmi *factfile*

Born: 13.6.1897, Turku
Died: 2.10.1973
Country: Finland
Olympic record: 1920: 10,000m gold, cross-country gold, cross-country team gold, 5,000m silver. 1924: 1,500m gold, 3,000m team gold, 5,000m gold, cross-country gold, cross-country team gold. 1928: 10,000m gold, 3,000m steeplechase silver, 5,000m silver

1928 IX OLYMPIADE AMSTERDAM

rest of the race by the side of Duquesne and once at the finishing line offered him first place. Duquesne declined, but the gesture showed that, though competitive, Nurmi never lost sight of Olympic ideals.

He went on to win a gold in the 10,000 metres and silver in the 5,000 metres and the steeplechase to take his overall tally to twelve medals, including nine gold and three silver.

'Babe' grows up
Los Angeles 1932

"Before I was ever in my teens, I knew exactly what I wanted to be when I grew up. My goal was to be the greatest athlete that ever lived."
Mildred 'Babe' Didrikson

The tenth Olympic Games in Los Angeles came at a bad time with the world gripped by depression. Less than 1,500 athletes took part. For many, however, all thoughts of depression were lifted by the performances of Mildred Didrikson.

The 18-year-old went into the Games as a typist from Texas but emerged as a great sporting hero. Nicknamed "Babe" at school after Babe Ruth, due to her prowess in baseball, she also excelled at basketball before deciding to concentrate on athletics for the forthcoming Olympics. She qualified to compete in eight events but was allowed to take part in only three. She subsequently won gold in the javelin and

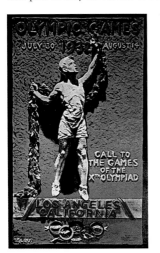

Mildred Didrikson winning the 80 metres hurdles in 1932. She was to be voted one of the century's greatest female athletes

Didrikson *factfile*

Born: 26.6.1914, Port Arthur, Texas
Died: 27.9.1956
Country: USA
Olympic record: 1932: 80m hurdles gold, javelin gold, high jump silver

80 metres hurdles but only received silver in the high jump despite breaking the world record. Her compatriot, Jean Shiley, jumped the same height, 5ft 5in, but was awarded the gold because of what the judges considered a 'better' jumping technique. In a gesture that once again summed up the Olympic spirit between competitors, the two athletes had the medals cut in half and joined the gold and silver halves together.

After the Games, Babe Didrikson went on to dominate the world of golf under her married name of Zaharias and in 1950 was voted the greatest female athlete of the first half of the century. Not many would argue against her being the greatest female athlete of all time.

Mixed-up girl
Los Angeles 1932

Helen Stephens, left, of the USA is congratulated by Stella Walsh (Stanislawa Walasiewicz) of Poland after Stephens set a new world record in winning the women's 100 metres at the 1936 Olympics

Born in Poland in 1911, Stanislawa Walasiewicz moved with her family to America at the age of two. As she started school in Cleveland, she changed her name to Stella Walsh. It was also at this point that she started to show great promise as a sprinter.

Nineteen years after arriving in America, Walsh entered the Los Angeles Olympics but competed for Poland rather than her adopted country. She went on to win the gold after a close finish in which second-placed Hilda Strike of Canada was accredited with the same time. It was after the race, however, that the controversy began. Many of the athletes in the race started to comment about Walsh's athletic, almost masculine, build. But no official complaint was made and Walsh went back to Ohio with the gold medal.

Four years later, Walsh again ran in the 100 metres under the Polish flag but was beaten into second place by America's Helen Stephens. Ironically, a handful of the Polish press accused Stephens of being a man and the Missouri farm girl had to endure a gender test. She passed.

In 1980, the story took another twist when Stella Walsh was gunned down and killed in Cleveland. A post-mortem revealed that Walsh suffered from the rare condition known as "mosaicism". This meant that Walsh actually possessed a mostly male chromosome balance. Despite this, the androgynous Walsh is still widely regarded as a great Olympic athlete.

15

Hockey team skates to surprise victory

Garmisch-Partenkirchen 1936

The Winter Olympics held in the neighbouring towns of Garmisch and Partenkirchen in the Bavarian Alps went a long way to securing the German's hold on the summer Olympics. Many countries argued that the Nazi regime should not be given the Olympics but the apparent success of these Games seemed to smooth over any real fears. Although only German photographers were allowed to cover the action, the lucky few who did get to report on the Games were witness to one of the biggest shocks of this or any other Winter Olympics.

The Canadians had dominated the ice hockey event ever since the first Winter Olympics in 1924 and no-one seriously thought that anyone would break their stranglehold. They didn't, however, count on a bunch of Canadian rejects with British parentage who opted to play for the country of their forefathers. The link was so tenuous with some of the players that two of them were banned due to dubious eligibility and were only reinstated shortly before the first game. The team went on to beat the Canadians 2-1 to leave them needing just a draw against the USA in their final match. Despite an onslaught from the American team and three periods of extra time, the British defence held firm for a goalless draw and the point they needed for an unlikely victory.

The 'British' hockey team that triumphed over Canada and the Unites States. Some of the players' links with the UK were highly tenuous

Garmisch 1936 *medals*

	Gold	Silver	Bronze
1. Norway	7	5	3
2. Germany	3	3	—
3. Sweden	2	2	3
4. Finland	1	2	3
5. Switzerland	1	2	—
7. Great Britain	1	1	1

Hitler humbled
Berlin 1936

The Berlin Olympics are one of the most famous, or infamous, Olympic Games of all time depending on how you look at it. On the one hand you have the remarkable achievements of Jesse Owens, but on the other the racial propaganda of Adolf Hitler.

Berlin was awarded the privilege of hosting the 1936 Olympics five years previously when the Olympic committee could not have foreseen the rise of the Nazi party. The Games were actually a great success, and in true military style very well organised but Hitler's Aryan ideals were never far below the surface. The Americans were

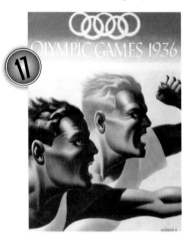

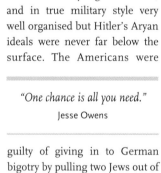

> *"One chance is all you need."*
> Jesse Owens

guilty of giving in to German bigotry by pulling two Jews out of the sprint relay team. One man who did compete, though, was the 22-year-old black athlete from Cleveland, Jesse Owens.

The previous year, he broke five world records and equalled another in the space of 45 minutes. Much to Hitler's chagrin he brought this form to Europe with him. He competed in four events – the 100 metres, 200 metres, long jump and 4x100 metres relay – winning gold in all. German Luz Long put

Owens *factfile*

Born: 12.9.1913, Danville, Ala
Died: 1982
Country: USA
Olympic record: 1936: 100m gold, 200m gold, 4x100m relay gold, long jump gold

Owens on his way to another gold. The watching Adolf Hitler was appalled

up a fight in the long jump and during the competition, against Nazi policy, befriended Owens. The two remained lifelong pals.

Hitler, of course, had no plans to do likewise and wouldn't even shake Owens's hand. The American famously quipped: "I didn't come here to shake hands anyway." Not many people upstaged Adolf Hitler at the height of his powers but in the summer of 1936 Jesse Owens did just that in spectacular fashion. But it is as one of the greatest-ever Olympians that he will be forever famed.

The Olympics returned after a break of 12 years due to the Second World War. London was the venue but many athletes had to bring their own food because of the rationing that still existed in Britain at the time. Despite this, more than 4,000 competitors took part and the Olympic movement was back on track.

As in Los Angeles in 1932, the biggest hero to emerge was a woman. Fanny Blankers-Koen was a 30-year-old mother of two when she competed in the London Olympics. The Dutch athlete had shown great promise competing in Berlin as an 18-year-old but many had thought her chance had passed when the next two Olympics were cancelled. If anyone thought she was past her best they were to be proven dramatically wrong as the "flying housewife" went on to emulate the feat of Jesse Owens and win four gold medals.

Blankers-Koen faced a tough task as, with heats and finals, she competed eleven times in eight days. But she won golds in the 100 metres, 200 metres, 80 metres hurdles and the 4x100 metres relay. Her two biggest

A heroine for a new age

London 1948

scares came in the hurdles, where British athlete Maureen Gardner ran her close, and the relay in which the Australian team held a big lead going into the last leg. Fanny Blankers-Koen managed to overhaul Joyce King of Australia with inches to spare and won by just one tenth of a second. The Olympics had found its first post-war heroine.

Maureen Gardner, right, second in the 80 metres hurdles final of the 1948 Olympics, congratulates the winner, Francina 'Fanny' Blankers-Koen (right, above)

Blankers-Koen *factfile*

Born: 26.4.1918, Amsterdam
Country: Holland
Olympic record: 1936: 4x100m relay fifth, high jump sixth. 1948: 100m gold, 200m gold, 80m hurdles gold, 4x100m relay gold

Teenage superstar
London 1948

If Fanny Blankers-Koen was the female hero of the London Olympics, then American Bob Mathias was undoubtedly the biggest male star. At 17 years and 263 days, he became the youngest-ever winner of an Olympic track and field gold medal. More impressively, his victory came in the toughest event of all, the decathlon. Consisting of 10 track and field events over two days, the decathlon is the ultimate test for an athlete. Mathias seemed to take to it with natural ease.

Just a few months before the Olympics, his high school track coach, little realising how good his foresight would prove, suggested that Mathias should try the decathlon. The young Californian proceeded to sweep aside the opposition in London to become a very popular gold medallist.

Mathias went on to dominate the event and was the first athlete to retain the decathlon gold medal four years later. He remained unbeaten throughout his 12-year career but was stopped from winning a golden hat-trick after he appeared in a film about his career in 1953. The International Olympic Committee immediately classed him as a professional and banned him from the 1956 Olympic competition where no one was seriously expected to beat him.

Mathias *factfile*

Born: 17.11.1930, Tulare, Cal
Country: USA
Olympic record: 1948: decathlon gold
1952: decathlon gold

Bob Mathias crossing the finishing line of the 1,500 metres at the London Olympics on his way to decathlon glory.
Left: In action at the 1952 Helsinki Games where he retained his gold medal

Zatopek leads the 5,000m final into the home straight. Britain's Chris Chataway, fourth, crashes out

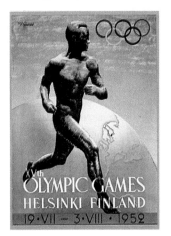

Zatopek factfile

Born: 19.9.1922, Koprivnice
Country: Czechoslovakia
Olympic record:
1948: 10,000m gold, 5,000m silver. 1952: 5,000m gold, 10,000m gold, marathon gold. 1956: marathon sixth

Keeping it in the family: Czech Olympic champions Emil Zatopek and his wife Dana Zatopkova, above, show off the four gold medals that they won at the 1952 Helsinki Games

Zatopek checks in
Helsinki 1952

The 1952 Olympics in Finland were opened by the great Olympic champion and national hero Paavo Nurmi, who had helped Finland dominate long-distance running before the war. So it was fitting that these Games would eventually belong to another long distance runner, Emil Zatopek.

Four years earlier, the Czech runner had won a gold medal in the 10,000 metres and silver in the 5,000 metres, but in Helsinki he was in his prime and had decided to enter the marathon as well as the two track events. No one had ever won all three events in the same Games but Zatopek got off to a great start by regaining his 10,000 metres crown with ease.

The 5,000 metres wasn't so easy and on the last bend he had to sprint round four runners before taking the gold by just one second.

Three days later, the Czech entered his first ever marathon in his third gold medal attempt of the Games. He started out cautiously and stayed close to experienced marathon runners. The "Czech Express" soon found the going too slow, however, and set off at his own pace. He proceeded to destroy a world-class field and took the gold medal in an Olympic record time of 2 hours and 23.04 minutes.

When later asked what his marathon debut was like, he simply replied: "Boring." Not to be upstaged, his wife, Dana, took gold in the javelin to top off a successful Games. No one could describe the Zatopek family as boring.

Britain salutes the Colonel
Helsinki 1952

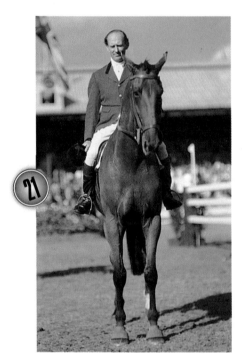

Up and over: Colonel Harry Llewellyn, captain of the British equestrian team, riding Foxhunter during the showjumping event at the Helsinki Games. Far left: Taking a bow at the medal ceremony

The Helsinki Games of 1952 may have been a great success in general but they looked like turning out to be an unparalleled disaster for Great Britain. Until an hour before the end of the Games Britain was in danger for the first time ever of leaving without winning a gold medal.

The saviour came in the shape of Colonel Harry Llewellyn and his horse Foxhunter.

The Great Britain showjumping team were slightly behind Chile going into the last round, where Llewellyn needed to jump a clear round for the title to go to Britain.

With just 15 minutes to go before the final ceremony, Llewellyn and Foxhunter showed great nerve and cleared the course perfectly, beating Chile to the Prix de Nations title and giving Britain its only gold of the Games.

Helsinki 1952 *medals*

	Gold	Silver	Bronze
1. USA	40	19	17
2. USSR	22	30	19
3. Hungary	16	10	16
4. Sweden	12	12	10
5. Italy	8	9	4

Aussie girls go for it
Helsinki 1952

"You have to be part of an Olympic team to fully realise the significance of competing in the greatest sporting event in the world. I think the tragedy is that the innocence has gone."
Marjorie Jackson

Crossing the line: Marjorie Jackson of Australia winning the women's 200 metres final at the Helsinki Olympics

The Helsinki Games saw the birth of Australian women's athletics as a world force with the team taking three gold and one bronze medal on the track. This was mainly due to two athletes, Shirley Strickland and Marjorie Jackson. Shirley had won a silver and two bronze medals in London four years earlier, and added to these with a gold and another bronze in Helsinki. The real star of these Games, however, was Jackson. The New South Wales sprinter, known as the Lithgow Flash, became the first Australian female to win a track and field gold medal. She did in fact go one better and won two golds, taking first place in both sprint races.

The 21-year-old won both races with relative ease to confirm her status as the world's premier sprinter. She entered the Olympics as the world record-holder over 100 metres and looked in no trouble during the race, winning in a new world record time of 11.5 seconds. The 200 metres was won by half a second over the Dutch athlete Bertha Brouwer as Jackson became the first Australian since Eddie Flack in 1896 to win an athletics gold medal. The only disappointment came in the 4x100 metres relay. Despite a strong line-up, the Australians finished unplaced. But Strickland and particularly Jackson had set the standards for Australian female athletes, whose time would surely come. Marjorie Jackson, however, would not be a part of it. She retired prematurely the next year at the age of 22.

The Blitz from Kitz

Cortina d'Ampezzo 1956

The Italian town of Cortina d'Ampezzo had waited 12 years to host the Winter Olympics – they were initially due to host the cancelled Games of 1944 – so they planned to make the most of them.

Located in the Dolomite mountains in northern Italy, the Games were almost doomed before they began, however, because of unseasonably mild weather that resulted in a lack of snow. But it finally came on the opening day.

Despite the early scare, the Games turned out to be a huge success, no more so than for Austrian skier Toni Sailer. Amongst the most watched events at the Games were the Alpine skiing events in which the 20-year-old from Kitzbuhel excelled marvellously.

Known as the "Blitz from Kitz", Sailer lived up to his nickname, taking the gold medal in all three competitions in blistering fashion. He won the downhill event by three and a half seconds, the slalom by four seconds and the giant slalom by a massive six seconds.

The Alpine events were relatively new to Olympic competition but Toni Sailer's style of skiing in front of live television cameras meant they would become one of the most popular events of the Winter Games. He also started the trend for great Alpine skiers in his own country.

Toni Sailer swoops downhill to win his third gold of the 1956 Games

Sailer *factfile*

Born: 17.11.1935, Kitzbuhel
Country: Austria
Olympic record: 1956: downhill gold, slalom gold, giant slalom gold

OLYMPIC GAMES

MELBOURNE
22 NOV–8 DEC
1956

In 1956, Melbourne was the first city south of the equator to host the Olympic Games. This proved a problem for some athletes as they couldn't afford the travel costs to acclimatise and the late opening of the Games, to coincide with the Australian summer, meant athletes had to retain their peak fitness over a longer period than usual. Despite this the Games were a great success.

And if Helsinki had seen the birth of Australian women's athletics then, fittingly, in Melbourne it came of age. In the absence of the Australian hero of the previous Games, Marjorie Jackson, the host nation's hopes rested on a new starlet, Betty Cuthbert. At only 18 years of age, it was a big burden to

Cuthbert *factfile*

Born: 20.4.1938, Merrylands, NSW
Country: Australia
Olympic record: 1956: 100m gold,
200m gold, 4x100m relay gold
1964: 400m gold

Beat that!: Betty Cuthbert wins the 200 metres from Christa Stubnik of Germany and Marlene Mathews of Australia

Christa Stubnick, second, and fellow Australian Marlene Matthews, third. With the shorter race won, the 200 metres caused no problems and the top three placings were identical to those in the 100 metres. Cuthbert was to run the anchor leg in her third attempt at gold in the 4x100 metres relay. A photo-finish was needed to separate her from British athlete Heather Armitage but to the delight of the crowd, the result was in no doubt and Cuthbert had won a hat-trick of golds to become the darling of the Games.

Four years later, she was denied the opportunity to add to her medal collection through injury, but she returned in Tokyo in 1964 to became part of a rare band of athletes who have won a gold medal in four different track events. In Japan, she concentrated her efforts on the 400 metres and despite being drawn in the inside lane, managed to win her fourth gold medal. She became known as the "Golden Girl" and is revered as one of Australia's great Olympians.

A real belter, Betty

Melbourne 1956

bear, but the young athlete from Sydney quite literally took it all in her stride. With a unique running style – high driving knee action, long stride and mouth wide open – she would become one of the most renowned Australian athletes of the century – even if she went into her first final, the 100 metres, lacking confidence because her favourite event was the 200 metres. But she screamed to victory in 11.5 seconds ahead of the German

25

Strickland went on to win the 80 metres hurdles title in Helsinki and as the holder she was one of the favourites in the 1956 final, despite then being in her 30s.

On the day, the crowd turned up wanting to see a home victory. Strickland did not let them down. She retained her gold medal by edging out Gisela Kohler of Germany into second place, with Norma Thrower, another Australian, coming third.

Strickland then ran the first leg as part of the successful 4x100 metres relay team in a fitting finale to the Melbourne Olympics for the Australian women and, on a personal level, to end her own career at the top.

Shirley then retired having won three gold, a silver and three bronze medals in 12 years.

Left: Strickland and Kohler (right) after their 80 metres hurdles duel, above

Strickland strides out
Melbourne 1956

If Betty Cuthbert played the role of the young prodigy in Melbourne, then she had her perfect foil in Shirley Strickland. The 31-year-old from Guildford, Western Australia, was already a veteran of two Olympics before competing in her own country. Primarily a hurdles expert, she was still quick enough along the flat to warrant a place in the relay team which she had been a part of in the two previous Olympics, winning a silver medal in London.

Also in London, she won the bronze medal in the 80 metres hurdles, giving a hint of what was to come.

Strickland *factfile*

Born: 18.7.1925, Guildford, WA
Country: Australia
Olympic record: 1948: 4x100m relay silver, 80m hurdles bronze, 100m bronze, 200m fourth. 1952: 80m hurdles gold, 100m bronze, 4x100m relay fifth. 1956: 80m hurdles gold, 4x100m relay gold

Anita's a splash hit
Rome 1960

JEUX DE LA XVII OLYMPIADE
ROMA   25.VIII-11.IX

I f the Italian town of Cortina d'Amprezzo found it hard waiting 12 years to host the Winter Olympics, then the Italian capital must have found it agonising, as it had to wait 52 years. Originally due to host the 1908 Olympics, the eruption of Mount Vesuvius meant those Games were moved to London. Most people agreed, however, it was well worth the wait once the 1960 Olympics got under way. Despite the stifling Mediterranean heat, the Games were a great success and were the first to enjoy total TV coverage. Athletes became national heroes overnight – which is what happened to Anita Lonsbrough, a 19-year-old clerk from Huddersfield.

The Americans dominated the swimming pool but it was a German, Wiltrud Urselmann, who pushed Lonsbrough close in the 200 metres breaststroke. The British teenager was forced to break the world record to claim the gold in a time of 2 minutes 49.5 seconds.

This was only the third time a British woman had won an individual swimming gold medal. Lonsbrough returned to her job in Huddersfield as a household name thanks to the power of television.

Lonsbrough *factfile*

Born: 10.8.1941 Huddersfield
Country: England
Olympic record: 1960: 200m breaststroke gold

Hands up: Anita Lonsbrough after winning her gold medal in Rome

Wilma's miracle
Rome 1960

With the Rome Games enjoying total TV coverage, viewers round the world were able to watch the remarkable story of Wilma Rudolph unfold. Born in Tennessee in 1940, she was the 20th of 22 children. A very ill child, she contracted polio at an early age, which resulted in the temporary loss of feeling in her left leg. Doctors said she wouldn't be able to walk unaided again but with the help of her large family Wilma proved everyone wrong.

Still, it wasn't until the age of 11 that she was fully able to walk without a leg brace. Just five years later, Rudolph represented the USA at the Melbourne Olympics, winning a bronze medal with the 4x100 metres relay team. But it was in Rome that she really excelled. By winning the 100 metres, 200 metres and 4x100 metres relay, she became the first American woman to win three track and field gold medals at the same Olympics. The two individual races were won with ease, but the relay was a close call. The US team had a problem with a baton change so Rudolph had to come from way behind on the final leg. With the finishing line approaching, she surged past Jutta Heine of Germany for a famous victory to delight the watching millions.

"My mother taught me very early to believe I could achieve any accomplishment I wanted to. The first was to walk without braces."
Wilma Rudolph

Left: Wilma Rudolph, the girl they said would never walk unaided, winning the 100m from Dorothy Hyman. **Right:** Rudolph celebrates winning the 200m with Hyman (silver) and Jutta Heine (bronze)

Rudolph *factfile*

Born: 23.6.1940 Clarksville, Tennessee
Died: 12.11.1994 Nashville, Tennessee
Country: USA
Olympic record: 1956: 4x100m relay bronze. 1960: 100m gold, 200m gold, 4x100m gold

Enter the Greatest
Rome 1960

The Rome Olympics were to be the first time the world witnessed the magical talents of Cassius Clay. He first boxed at the age of 12 – and won. His trainer then encouraged Clay to look towards taking part in the Olympics, which if he won would give him an automatic top ten ranking in the world, rather than fighting his way up through the professional ranks.

After a successful amateur career, 18-year-old Clay reluctantly set off for Rome. He was scared of flying. Once in the Eternal City, it appeared that the flight was the only thing that scared him. He floated and stung his way past his opponents with a combination of power,

To make America the greatest is my goal
So I beat the Russian, and I beat the Pole
And for the USA won the Medal of Gold
Italians said "You're greater than Cassius of old"
We like your name, we like your game
So make Rome your home if you will
I said I appreciate your kind hospitality
But the USA is my country still
Cause they waiting to welcome me in Louisville.

Clay's first published poem,
written on his return from Rome

28

precision and immense speed that was rarely seen in the 178-pound light heavyweight division. In the final, he met the three-times European champion, Zbigniew Pietrzykowski. The experienced Pole, however, had never come up against anyone like Clay and the young American won the contest with a unanimous decision.

Many who watched Clay power his way to victory sensed they had seen the start of something special They were not wrong. Clay was to become Muhammad Ali and, many agreed, quite simply The Greatest.

Now for the big time: The smiling Cassius Clay, who took gold, towers over his fellow medal-winners

"It's lack of faith that makes people afraid of meeting challenges, and I believe in myself."
Cassius Clay

Clay *factfile*

Born: 17.1.1942 **Country:** USA
Cassius Clay changed his name to Muhammad Ali in 1965. He held the world heavyweight title between Feb 1964 - Feb 1970, Oct 1974 - Feb 1978, Sep 1978 - Jun 1979.
Professional record:
Bouts: 61 **Won:** 56 **Lost:** 5 **KO's:** 37

Mighty Mouse walks it
Rome 1960

Thompson *factfile*

Born: 20.1.33, Hillingdon, Middlesex
Country: England
Olympic record: 1960: 50km walk gold

Left: Don Thompson on a victory roll
and, above, with co-medal winners
Ljunggren of Sweden and Pamich of Italy

With the Games in Rome taking place at the height of summer, most British athletes couldn't produce their best performances as they struggled to acclimatise to the conditions. One man who didn't have any such problems, however, was Don Thompson, thanks to an ingenious training regime. The 'Mighty Mouse' from Middlesex had, for months, been preparing himself for the sweltering conditions of the Eternal City at home in the south of England. He filled the bath full of hot water and practised in the steam-filled bathroom in order to recreate the conditions that would present themselves in Rome. This unorthodox method worked brilliantly as he finished 17 seconds ahead of the Swede John Ljunggren in the punishing 50 kilometre walk, to become the only British athlete to win a track and field gold medal at these Games.

30

Elliott *factfile*

Born: 1938, Western Australia
Country: Australia
Olympic record: 1960: 1500m gold

Herb Elliot winning the final of the 1500 metres and setting a new world record of 3 minutes 35.6 seconds

The spice of Herb
Rome 1960

"I would say the Olympics are more exciting today because live television brings the excitement of the Games to the world. In 1960 it took three days for the tape to arrive back in Australia."

Herb Elliott

The middle-distance runner Herb Elliott was already a hero in his native Australia before the Rome Olympics and would become a household name throughout the world after his performance on the track.

The 22-year-old from Western Australia was unbeaten over 1500 metres coming into the Games and so was the hot favourite to take gold. And he did it in style. As the bell rang to announce the final lap, the race was still up for grabs. This is where Elliott made his decisive move and literally sprinted the remaining 400 metres to take the gold and in the process smash the world record. The Frenchman Michel Jazy finished three seconds behind in second place. The popular Antipodean had taken a world-class field apart in what is still regarded as one of the most decisive victories in Olympic history. Elliott remained unbeaten over 1500 metres throughout his career and is still thought of as one of Australia's most popular Olympians.

The marathon in the Rome Olympics was to hold the record of many firsts. It was the first to be run at night and was also the first not to start or finish in the stadium. It would also become the race that saw the first-ever black African gold medallist.

The 28-year-old Abebe Bikila had come to the Olympics virtually unknown outside his native Ethiopia. But he produced an outstanding marathon victory, smashing the world record with a time of 2 hours 15

The barefoot racer
Rome 1960

minutes and 16 seconds. Astonishingly, Bikila did the whole thing in his bare feet. And he felt that his victory was so easy that he said after the race: "I could have gone round again without any difficulty."

Four years later in Tokyo, he became the first athlete to successfully defend the Olympic marathon title. This time he wore shoes, but only six weeks earlier he had had an appendix operation.

Bikila was to be paralysed from the waist down in a car accident but even then competed as an archer in the paraplegic Games. But it is running barefoot to victory down a torchlit Appian Way in 1960 that he will be remembered.

Bikila *factfile*

Born: 7.8.1932, Mout
Died: 25.10.1973
Country: Ethiopia
Olympic record: 1960: marathon gold. 1964: marathon gold

Top: Celebrations and, left, barefoot Ethiopian athlete Abebe Bikila strides to marathon fame

Marvellous Mary
Tokyo 1964

In 1964, Japan hosted the Olympic Games. And did so superbly. The overall organisation and standard of the Games were top-class and the athletes rose to the occasion by breaking many world records

One of the record breakers was British runner Mary Rand. She had competed four years earlier in Rome but had come away unluckily empty-handed. In the 80 metres hurdles she missed out on a medal by just one tenth of a second. In the 4x100 metres relay, the team lost the baton, and in the long jump she leaped 6.33 metres in qualifying – good enough for silver – but when it mattered in the final she could only manage 6.01 metres.

Four years of hard work saw her return to the Olympics in Tokyo determined to succeed. A great all-round athlete at the peak of her career, she won a bronze medal in the 4x100 metres relay, a silver in the pentathlon and managed to complete the set by winning gold in the long jump.

Her leap of 6.76 metres was a new world record and more than made up for the disappointments of Rome.

All-round athlete Mary Rand leaps for gold at Tokyo

TOKYO ● 1964

Rand *factfile*

Born: 1940
Country: England
Olympic record: 1960: 80m hurdles fourth. 1964: long jump gold, pentathlon silver, 4x100m relay bronze

32

Dawn of a golden day
Tokyo 1964

Fraser *factfile*

Born: 4.9.1937, Balmain, NSW
Country: Australia
Olympic record: 1956: 100m
freestyle gold, 4x100m freestyle relay
gold, 400m freestyle silver
1960: 100m freestyle gold, 4x100m
freestyle relay silver, 4x100m medley
relay silver, 400m freestyle fifth
1964: 100m freestyle gold,
4x100m freestyle relay silver,
400m freestyle fourth

**Good going: Dawn Fraser's Tokyo
triumph meant she was the second
swimmer to win three consecutive
gold medals in the same event**

**Above: Bemedalled Davies takes the applause.
Right: Pausing for a picture at a training session.
Far right: The 26ft five-and-a-half inch jump in
pouring rain to win the gold medal in Tokyo**

Tokyo 1964 *medals*

	Gold	Silver	Bronze
1. USA	36	28	28
2. USSR	30	31	35
3. Japan	16	5	8
4. Germany	10	21	19
5. Italy	10	10	7

Dawn Fraser is still regarded as one of Australia's greatest female athletes and her Olympic record is testimony to this. Born in New South Wales in 1937, she suffered from bronchial asthma throughout her career but this didn't prevent her from becoming one of the greatest female swimmers of all time.

She competed in the Melbourne Olympics at the age of 19, picking up two golds and one silver medal. In Rome, she went on to win another gold and two more silver medals before her finest hour in Tokyo.

The final of the 100 metres freestyle was a close affair but Fraser managed to just outstretch American Sharon Stouder by four tenths of a second in a new Olympic record time of 59.5 seconds. This victory meant that Fraser was only the second swimmer in history to win three consecutive gold medals in the same event. It was a feat that Fraser and the whole of Australia were proud of.

Leap to stardom
Tokyo 1964

The Tokyo Olympic Games were to see their fair share of upsets along the way, and none more so than in the long jump event. The young British athlete Lynn Davies came into the Games as the underdog behind American athlete and current Olympic champion Ralph Boston. In the previous Games, Boston had just managed to beat his countryman Irvin Roberson by a quarter of an inch, but this time it was the American's turn to just miss out on gold.

In the qualifying round, Davies was almost eliminated. His coach Ron Pickering felt optimistic, however, that he could snatch a bronze medal. On the day of the final, the weather had turned for the worse and it was Davies who equipped himself best to the cold, wet and windy conditions. On his fifth attempt he produced a personal best of 8.07 metres, which was also a British record. Davies's leap was just 4 centimetres longer than that of Boston, as he became the first British male to win a gold medal in this event.

This elevated the Welshman to sporting star status throughout Britain in what was becoming a successful Olympic campaign for the country.

Davies *factfile*

Born: 1942
Country: Wales
Olympic record: 1964: long jump gold.
1968: long jump ninth

34

That's my girl
Tokyo 1964

35

Team spirit: Ann Packer of Great Britain, winner of the 800 metres final, gives her boyfriend, Robbie Brightwell, captain of the British team, a big hug

If Lynn Davies became the surprise male track and field hero of the Tokyo Olympics then Ann Packer was his equivalent in the female team. In the 400 metres, she narrowly lost to the great Australian athlete Betty Cuthbert by just two tenths of a second and had to be content with a silver medal. But this made her even more determined to succeed in the 800 metres. Up against a world-class field, Packer, who had only run this distance seven times, was never seriously expected to take gold but she ran a perfect race to finish just under a second faster than France's Maryvonne Dupureur in 2 minutes 1.1 seconds. Her joyful post-victory embrace with boyfriend Robbie Brightwell, himself a silver medallist with the 4×400 metres relay team, is one of the enduring images of those Games for British supporters.

Packer *factfile*

Born: 1942
Country: England
Olympic record: 1964:
800m gold, 400m silver

Smokin' Joe's secret

Tokyo 1964

Frazier *factfile*

Born: 12.1.1944, Beaufort, S.C.
Country: USA
Frazier was crowned the undisputed champion of the world in 1970 when he knocked out Jimmy Ellis in the 4th round.
Professional record: Bouts: 37 **Won:** 32
Lost: 4 **Drawn:** 1 **KO's:** 27

36

Going down: Joe Frazier sends one of his early rivals to the canvas during his campaign to win the heavyweight gold medal at the 1964 Olympics

Smokin' Joe Frazier very nearly didn't make it to the Tokyo Olympics. He lost in the U.S. Olympic trials to Buster Mathis on a points decision. However, Mathis was forced to withdraw due to a hand injury and Frazier never looked back. In the Olympics, he powered his way past his first three opponents in the heavyweight division. This came at a price, however, when he realised he had broken his right hand. It seemed ironic that an injured hand, the same injury that stopped Mathis going to the Olympics, was going to scupper Frazier's moment of glory.

Frazier then displayed the courage that would epitomise his career. He kept the injury a secret from the team doctors and fought on in the final. Relying on his famous left hook, he managed to beat the German Hans Huber on a split decision to win a very painful gold medal.

Frazier went on to enjoy a very successful professional boxing career in the sport's golden age that also included Olympic gold medallists Muhammad Ali and George Foreman.

Mystery on the slopes
Grenoble 1968

37

Left: Jean-Claude Killy shows his determination battling it out in the slalom at Grenoble in the 1968 Winter Olympics.
Above: Killy (left) and Guy Perillat celebrate their performances in the men's downhill ski event. Unstoppable Killy won the gold medal and Perillat finished second to take the silver

The Winter Olympics of 1968 returned to the French Alps after an absence of 20 years and local skiing hero Jean-Claude Killy was the star attraction. He emulated the feat of famous Austrian Toni Sailer by winning all three Alpine skiing events, to the delight of the partisan crowd. The French skier's achievement was less convincing than the Austrian's, however, his final victory coming amid much controversy.

Killy had developed a new style of skiing by placing his feet wider apart to gain more balance. This certainly worked in the giant slalom where he beat Swiss skier Willy Favre into second place by two seconds. The downhill event was much closer with Killy taking gold by just one tenth of a second over his countryman Guy Perillat. It was in the third event that controversy reigned. The slalom took place in fog as Killy battled it out with Austrian hero Karl Schranz. Killy was leading when Schranz set off on his run. The Austrian seemed to be going well when he slid to a halt in the middle of the course. He then claimed that a figure dressed in black had appeared and hindered his momentum.

The judges agreed to let him ski again, as they could see no other reason for the premature halt. Schranz then clocked up a winning time in his second run and was proclaimed the champion. But one observant judge announced that Schranz had missed a couple of gates on his first run before the intervention of the mystery man. The Austrian was subsequently disqualified amid much recrimination and Killy took his third gold medal of the Games to became an even greater national hero.

Killy *factfile*

Born: 30.8.1943, St Cloud, Alsace
Country: France
Olympic record: 1964: giant slalom fifth, downhill 42nd, slalom disqualified 1968: giant slalom gold, downhill gold, slalom gold

Black Power on the world stage
Mexico City 1968

The Mexico Olympic Games seemed to sum up the mood of the late Sixties in the space of just two weeks. The stand-off in the Cold War was apparent as two separate German teams competed against each other amid much acrimony. The social problems in Mexico were highlighted when protesting students were shot at by army and police, and the racial problems in the USA were brought to the world's attention by two athletes.

Tommie Smith and John Carlos were relatively unknown before the 1968 Olympic Games but their actions on October 16 became one of the most enduring images of the century. These two talented athletes had considered boycotting the Games in sympathy with the black civil rights movement that was gathering pace in their homeland. Instead, they decided they would create more publicity by winning medals and making a demonstration on a world stage.

They both reached the 200 metres final and Smith went on to win with Carlos third.

The Australian Peter Norman separated them at the tape, taking the silver medal. It was at the medal ceremony that the two Americans let their protests be known. On the podium, as the Star Spangled Banner struck up, the two bemedalled athletes bowed their heads and raised their black gloved fists in salute to the Black Power movement in the United States.

The gesture made them recognised faces around the world and instant heroes to many in their own country. But the US Olympic committee banned the pair and sent them home. Thirty-two years on, some may feel that Smith and Carlos were hard done by.

Protest: The US 4 x 400 metres gold medal-winning team follow the example of Carlos and Smith, the 200 metres medal-winners. Both ceremonies were used for Black Power salutes

1968 MEXICO

Cold War showdown
Mexico City 1968

Mexico City 1968 *medals*

	Gold	Silver	Bronze
1. USA	45	28	34
2. USSR	29	32	30
3. Japan	11	7	7
4. Hungary	10	10	12
5. East Germany	9	9	7

Foreman *factfile*

Born: 10.1.1949, Marshall, Texas
Country: USA
Foreman held the world heavyweight title from
Jan 1973 - Oct 1974 and Nov 1994 - Nov 1997.
Professional record:
Bouts: 81 **Won:** 76 **Lost:** 5 **KO's:** 68

Victor: Big-hitter George Foreman takes gold

George Foreman went to the Mexico City Olympics to make a name for himself, just as Cassius Clay had done in Rome and Joe Frazier had in Tokyo. It would take something spectacular to top the previous two heavyweight victories achieved by these two great champions, but if anyone could do it, the big-hitting American George Foreman was the man.

With just 18 amateur bouts behind him, many thought Foreman wasn't ready for the Olympic Games. But they did not take into consideration his incredible punching power. Foreman powered his way through the early rounds in a way that caught the public's eye. His opponent in the final was Ionas Tschepulis of the Soviet Union. With the tensions of the Cold War ever present, this final seemed to take on an added edge for many people.

As it turned out, there was little excitement in the encounter. Foreman finished the one-sided bout within two rounds. With the punching power that would take him on to become the world heavyweight champion, Foreman battered the Russian into submission inside six minutes to take the gold medal in his final amateur outing.

Vera's protest
Mexico City 1968

Caslavska *factfile*

Born: 3.5.1942, Prague
Country: Czech Republic
Olympic record: 1960: gymnastics team silver, beam sixth. 1964: individual combined gold, vaults gold, beam gold, gymnastics team silver, parallel bars fifth, floor exercises sixth. 1968: individual combined gold, vaults gold, parallel bars gold, floor exercises gold, gymnastics team silver, beam silver

Vera Caslavska was already an Olympic champion going into the Mexico City Games. The Czech gymnast had won three gold medals in Tokyo four years previously but many thought the invasion of her homeland by Russian forces just a couple of months before the 1968 Games would be likely to affect her performance.

It transpired that it may well have been so, as she seemed to try even harder. The stylish athlete surpassed the high level of gymnastics she had produced in Tokyo and went on to take four gold medals. The crowd instantly took to her and she became the undoubted Queen of the Games. This manifested itself when, during the competition, she married the 1500 metres silver medallist from Tokyo Josef Odlozil. A crowd of 10,000 Mexicans surrounded the church to join in the celebrations and congratulate the popular champion.

Unfortunately, the Games ended on a sour note for Caslavska. The final score of the Soviet gymnast Larissa Petrik was altered just before the medal ceremony of the floor exercise, giving her a share of first place. Caslavska shared the podium with her without complaint but bowed her head during the Soviet anthem to show her disgust over that country's actions against her homeland. After she returned home she found that her political gesture had spelled the end of her gymnastic career. But she had won the nation's admiration.

Above and left: Vera Caslavska displays her remarkable gymnastic prowess at the 1968 Games. But political factors were to end her career

One giant leap...
Mexico City 1968

"Whatever you do, don't do it halfway."
Bob Beamon

The high altitude of Mexico City was something that caused concern for most of the participating nations in the 1968 Olympics. It was feared that the performance in the endurance events would suffer because of the conditions and that some competitors would have an advantage in the so-called explosive events. As it happened, most contestants trained at high altitude for months before the Games and were well prepared. And the Mexico City Olympics, fought out at an altitude of 7,000 feet, would see an unprecedented number of records broken.

The most famous record of them all was set by 20-year-old American long-jumper Bob Beamon. Going into the Games, Beamon was expected to slug it out with the two other favourites, Ralph Boston of the USA and Soviet athlete Igor Ter-Ovanesyan. In the qualifying round, however, it seemed that Beamon would not even reach the final as he fouled in his first two jumps. With one attempt left, Ralph Boston advised Beamon that if he took off one foot from the board he would still make the qualifying distance. Beamon did just that and qualified easily. If Boston had read up on his Olympic history, however, he might not have been so ready with his advice. In 1936, Luz Long had given the same advice to Jesse Owens.

In the final, Beamon broke all the records. In one jump he became the first man to leap further than 29 feet, when no one had even broken the 28-feet barrier. His jump of 29 feet two-and-a-half inches was untouchable. Second placed Klaus Beer, from East Germany', jumped just 26 feet 10-and-a-half inches.

Above: The 29ft jump that earned Bob Beamon his gold medal, above left

Born: 1946
Country: USA
Olympic record: 1968: long jump gold

The revolutionary Fosbury Flop
Mexico City 1968

*I*f it was argued that Mexico City's high altitude had contributed to Bob Beamon's remarkable gold medal in the long jump, then the same certainly could not be said of Dick Fosbury's victory in the high jump.

After struggling to reach anywhere near the height needed to compete at the top level, Fosbury decided to change his style. He came back with a bizarre technique that looked awkward and very dangerous but after a little practice was extremely effective.

Instead of diving over the bar in a forward motion and 'scissoring' his legs over it – the classic high-jump technique — Fosbury leapt backwards over the bar, flipping his legs up at the last moment. His fellow athletes were astounded. So were the millions watching on TV. Fosbury's coach commented: "If kids imitate him, he will wipe out an entire generation of high-jumpers because they will all have broken necks."

But Fosbury had the last laugh, taking the gold medal thanks to his courage and vision to try out this new technique. It became

known as the 'Fosbury Flop' and is the method used by all high-jumpers since the day this innovative athlete literally put his neck on the line.

Fosbury *factfile*

Born: 6.3.1947, Portland, Oregon
Country: USA
Olympic record: 1968: high jump gold

Putting his back into it: Dick Fosbury demonstrates his revolutionary medal-winning technique

Uncatchable Keino
Mexico City 1968

Kipchoge Keino's achievement at the 1968 Games was the start of a succession of great victories for Kenyans at the Olympics. At the age of 28, he was in his prime and the altitude proved no problem for him as he won the 1500 metres with ease. The second-placed athlete, Jim Ryun of the USA, finished a full three seconds behind. Keino then went on to compete in the 5,000 metres final. This race was much closer, Keino being beaten into second place by just two tenths of a second by the Tunisian Mohamed Gammoudi.

But the Kenyan policeman returned to the Olympics four years later to claim his second gold and silver medals. In the 1500 metres, he finished second to Finland's Pekka Vasala as the Finns became a world force again. In the steeplechase, he took the gold by beating his countryman Benjamin Jipcho by a full minute.

Above left: Kip Keino wins the 1,500 metres final at Mexico in a record time of 3 mins, 34.9 seconds and, above right, sets out on a celebratory lap of honour with a team-mate

Keino *factfile*

Born: 17.1.1940, Kipsano
Country: Kenya
Olympic record:
1964: 5,000m fifth.
1968: 1500m gold, 5,000m silver.
1972: 3,000m steeplechase gold, 1500m silver

Al's well in the end
Mexico City 1968

I f anyone epitomises the Olympic ideal then it is surely the American discus-thrower Al Oerter. To him, the Olympics seemed to mean everything and the Games invariably brought the best out of him. Throughout Olympic history, it seems no one rose to the occasion better than Oerter.

His remarkable record began in Melbourne in 1956 where, at the age of 20, he surprised everyone with an Olympic record throw of 56.36 metres to take his first gold medal. In Rome, he again broke the Olympic record, this time reaching 59.18 metres to win his second consecutive gold.

His hat-trick of victories came in Tokyo against the strongest of odds and doctor's orders. Just before the 1964 Games, he tore cartilages in his lower rib cage and was told not to train, never mind compete. But he was determined not to miss the Olympics and after discarding his bandages he threw the Discus more than 200 feet – six feet further than his nearest rival.

By the time the Mexico Olympics came round Oerter was 32 years old but still in good shape and was looking good for an unprecedented fourth consecutive gold medal. His first two throws, however, were not of his usual quality and many wondered if Oerter's supremacy had finally come to an end. On his third throw he slightly adjusted his technique and threw yet another Olympic record distance of 64.78 metres.

He duly won his fourth gold medal and ensured he would be remembered as one of the greatest of all Olympians.

Below: Discus-thrower Al Oerter in action at Rome and, right, seemingly looking to the heavens for inspiration

Oerter *factfile*

Born: 19.9.1936, Astoria, NY
Country: USA
Olympic record:
1956: discus gold. 1960: discus gold
1964: discus gold. 1968: discus gold

44

Hemery overcomes altitude hurdle

Mexico City 1968

Before the 1968 Games, many thought that the high altitude of Mexico City would cause great problems for British athletes. This meant that the majority of them took at least two months to acclimatise. One of these athletes was the blond 400 metres hurdler David Hemery. He was in good form going into the Games but a question mark remained on how he would cope with the conditions.

He reached the final comfortably and was drawn in lane six. This meant that his main rivals would be inside him and so he couldn't see their progress. Seemingly with this in mind he took off at his own pace. As a measure of his confidence, he kept the pace going and worried only about his own performance, rather than that of his opponents. He took the tape a second ahead of the German Gerhard Hennige.

The extra training had obviously paid off. Not only did Hemery win the gold medal comprehensively, in the process he also smashed the world record with a time of 48 minutes 12 seconds.

Left: David Hemery clears the final hurdle to take gold in the 400 metres hurdles final in Mexico.
Right: On the winner's podium sporting his gold medal

Hemery *factfile*

Born: 1944 **Country:** England
Olympic record: 1968: 400m hurdles gold. 1972: 4x400m relay silver, 400m hurdles bronze

München 1972 26.8.–10.9.

Shane shows spirit
Munich 1972

The Munich Olympics will always be remembered for a tragedy that made sport look irrelevant. Two Israeli athletes were killed by a band of 'Black September' Arab guerrillas who stormed the Olympic Village and took nine more Israelis hostage. All nine died less than 24 hours later in a gun battle in which a policeman and four terrorists were also shot dead.

The Games were suspended for two days but, despite the horror, sport still made its mark

The Australian swimmer Shane Gould was only 15 when she entered the Olympics. She was far from unknown, however, and the American team issued a challenge by wearing T-shirts with the legend: "All that glitters is not Gould".

The young swimmer from Brisbane was not fazed and she showed maturity beyond her years.

She entered five events, won three, and finished a close second and third in the other two. She set world records in the 200 and 400 metres freestyle and the 200 metres individual medley – making her the first woman to achieve that feat.

By the end of 1972, she held the world record for all freestyle events up to 1500 metres, but then turned professional at 16, robbing herself of the chance to compete in the following Olympics.

In the swim: Shane Gould powers through the water. She was the first woman to win three titles in record times

Born: 4.9.1956, Brisbane, Queensland
Country: Australia
Olympic record: 1972: 200m freestyle gold, 400m freestyle gold, 200m individual medley gold, 800m freestyle silver, 100m freestyle bronze

47

Spitz *factfile*

Seven-up Spitz

Munich 1972

"I'm trying to do the best I can. I'm not concerned with tomorrow, but with what goes on today."

Mark Spitz

Born: 10.2.1950, Modesto, Cal

Country: USA

Olympic record: 1968: 4x100m freestyle relay gold, 4x200m freestyle relay gold, 100m butterfly silver, 100m freestyle bronze. 1972: 100m freestyle gold, 200m freestyle gold, 100m butterfly gold, 200m butterfly gold, 4x100m freestyle relay gold, 4x200m freestyle gold, 4x100m medley relay gold

Stroke of genius: Mark Spitz competing in the 1972 Games where he would win seven gold medals

The relative failure of Mark Spitz at the 1968 Olympic Games had been a major talking point among sports fans in America after the Games. But no one was more disappointed than Spitz himself. This was to spur the disconsolate swimmer on for the following four years before he got the chance to make amends.

In Munich, Spitz was in a class of his own as he embarked on what could be considered the greatest Olympic performance of all time. He took part in seven events and came away with seven gold medals – the highest number ever won by an individual in one Olympic Games. Spitz's medals came in four individual races – the 100 and 200 metres freestyle and the 100 and 200 metres butterfly – and also in three team events, the 4x100 metres and 4x200 metres freestyle relays and the 4x100 metres medley relay. His achievements were all the more spectacular in that he broke the world record in every event that he contested.

Spitz had certainly laid the ghost of 1968.

Korbut's charisma
Munich 1972

"Don't be afraid if things seem difficult in the beginning. That's only the initial impression. The important thing is not to retreat; you have to master yourself."

Olga Korbut

Waif-like Russian gymnast Olga Korbut won the hearts of the world. The 17-year-old captured the imagination not only of spectators at the Games, but also of millions who were watching on television throughout the world. This popularity helped to raise the profile of gymnastics as an Olympic event and turned Olga into a global superstar.

Her grace and balance coupled with youthfulness and a radiant smile were a winning combination and instantly endeared her to the crowd. She went on to win three gold medals and one silver, despite only finishing seventh overall. Her victories came in the team event, the beam and the floor exercises. Her silver came for her prowess on the asymmetrical parallel bars.

Olga Korbut went on to take another gold medal and a silver at Montreal four years later, before turning to a lucrative professional career.

Top: 17-year-old Olga Korbut at the centre of attraction with her 1972 medal-winning teammates and, right, in action on the asymmetric bars

Korbut *factfile*

Born: 16.5.1955, Belarus
Country: USSR
Olympic record: 1972: gymnastics team gold, beam gold, floor exercises gold, parallel bars silver, vaults fourth. 1976: gymnastics team gold, beam silver, individual combined fifth, parallel bars fifth

49

Mary wins by smiles
Munich 1972

The 1972 Olympics were a big disappointment for Great Britain. The lacklustre performance was lifted, however, when the ever-smiling Mary Peters embarked on her third quest for a gold medal. The wait was to be more than worth it for the Northern Ireland athlete.

Peters competed in the pentathlon against a world-class field in which the West German Heide Rosendahl was the favourite. Rosendahl was a long-jump specialist, as well as an excellent all-round athlete. She had already won the long-jump gold before entering the pentathlon. Peters had her work cut out but she managed to grit her teeth and put in the performance of her life. The final event was the 200 metres in which Peters had to finish no more than 1.2 seconds behind Rosendahl and 0.4 seconds behind East German Burglinde

Pollak to take the gold. The result was a victory for Peters by just ten points – the margin of just one tenth of a second in that final race when Rosendahl came second.

This courageous victory was the only track and field gold medal won by a British athlete in Munich. Mary's popularity was confirmed when she won the 1972 BBC Sports Personality of the Year award.

Above: Mary Peters drives away at the start of the 200 metres and, above left, giving her all in the long jump

Peters *factfile*

Born: 1939
Country: Northern Ireland
Olympic record:
1964: pentathlon fourth
1968: pentathlon ninth
1972: pentathlon gold

Pushing the boat out
Munich 1972

Britain won only four gold medals at the Munich Olympics. Apart from the pentathlon triumph of Mary Peters, there were two golden victories in equestrian events and another in yachting.

The yachting gold was won by Rodney Pattisson and Christopher Davies in the Flying Dutchman Class. They managed to keep their nerve and beat the French team and the host nation into second and third respectively. This was Pattisson's second gold medal after he had come back from Mexico victorious four years earlier. He won that gold in the same class, but his partner on that occasion was Iain Macdonald-Smith. The pair beat off a strong challenge from the West Germans in central America.

With many of the more famous British athletes failing to perform at their best in Munich, it was up to the unsung heroes to ensure Britain didn't leave the Games empty-handed.

Rodney Pattisson was one of those who did not disappoint when it mattered most.

Golden yachtsman Rodney Pattisson is presented with an award by 84-year-old David Jacobs, a former Olympics gold medal winner who captained the British team in 1912

Pattisson *factfile*

Born: 5.8.1943, Campbelltown
Country: Scotland
Olympic record:
1968: Flying Dutchman gold
1972: Flying Dutchman gold
1976: Flying Dutchman silver

US upset by a Soviet slam-dunk
Munich 1972

Since the Berlin Olympics of 1936, the United States basketball team had won every gold medal and usually beat the Soviet Union in the final. It seemed unlikely that Munich would be an exception.

The two adversaries again battled it out, the USSR hoping finally to halt the USA's 62-game Olympic winning streak. They actually pushed them very close all through the game but with the clock ticking away, the USA held a slight advantage. It looked like it would be their eighth victory in a row. The clock was into the final seconds when the Soviet Union tried one

The USA have won 12 of the 15 golds competed for in basketball. The USSR (now Russia) have won two and Yugoslavia have won one

last attack. But the US defence was looking as strong as ever and it seemed there was no way through. Then against all the odds a long throw was attempted and went straight through the basket for one of the unlikeliest of victories.

Millions of TV viewers around the world watched the ensuing scenes – the Soviets running around in jubilation and the Americans slumped in disbelief.

This Soviet victory still remains one of the biggest upsets in Olympic history.

Wilkie makes waves
Montreal 1976

CANADA
1976

Wilkie *factfile*

Born: 8.3.1954 Colombo, Sri Lanka
Country: England
Olympic record:
1972: 200m breaststroke silver
1976: 200m breaststroke gold,
100m breaststroke silver

52

**Smiles at the medal ceremony for
David Wilkie after his record-breaking
gold medal swim (main picture)**

The 1976 Olympic Games in Montreal were hit by 22 African nations boycotting the event. This was due to the participation of New Zealand in the Games after they had earlier in the year sent a rugby team to apartheid South Africa. The loss of these nations was expected to affect the results on the track. But it was felt that swimming was one sport that would be unaffected.

The USA was expected to sweep the board in the pool regardless of any boycott. It would take something spectacular to break their dominance. But that something came in the form of British breaststroke specialist David Wilkie. In winning the 200 metres breaststroke gold he stopped the USA from winning all the male swimming events.

In the final he was up against John Hencken, who just beat Wilkie in the 100 metres breaststroke final. But in the 200 metres Wilkie took gold in 2 minutes 15.11 seconds, breaking the world record. Hencken was a full two seconds behind.

Nadia, superstar
Montreal 1976

"Hard work has made it easy. That is my secret. That is why I win."

I f Olga Korbut had caught the imagination of the public with her gymnastic displays in Munich, it was nothing to what Nadia Comaneci was about to achieve. The Romanian athlete was just 14 when she entered the Games but her youth did nothing to daunt the multi-talented gymnast.

Her performances were to change the face of gymnastics forever as she took the sport to new heights. Her score of 10 on the asymmetric bars was the first perfect score in Olympic history. She went on to repeat the feat a further four times as she won three gold, one silver and one bronze medal. Her three victories came in the beam, the asymmetric bars and the combined event.

She went on to win another two gold medals in Moscow four years later at the grand old age of 18.

Comaneci *factfile*

53

Born: 12.9.1961
Country: Romania
Olympic record: 1976: individual combined gold, beam gold, parallel bars gold, gymnastics team silver, floor exercises bronze, vaults fourth
1980: beam gold, floor exercises gold, individual combined silver, gymnastics team silver, vaults fifth

Perfect standing: 14-year-old Romanian gymnast Nadia Comaneci scored three maximum 10-out-of-10 scores at Montreal, the first perfect scores ever obtained by a gymnast in the history of the Olympics

Lasse, the long-distance runner
Montreal 1976

54

L asse Viren was already an Olympic hero going into the 1976 Games. He had revived the great Finnish long-distance running tradition set by Paavo Nurmi when he won both the 5,000 metres and 10,000 metres in Munich. His victory in the 10,000 metres was all the more remarkable as he fell at the midway stage. He picked himself up and won, breaking the world record by a second.

At the Montreal Olympics, he was attempting to retain both the 5,000 metres and 10,000 metres titles, something no one had ever achieved. The Finn was once again unbeatable as he strode to victory in both races to rewrite the record books and bring memories flooding back of the great Finnish long-distance runners from before the war.

A few days later, he entered the marathon looking for a hat-trick of victories. Though he only managed fifth in the 26-mile race, it was still a great run taking his earlier exploits into consideration. Despite this final disappointment, Lasse Viren had put Finnish long-distance running back on the Olympic map.

Showing the way: Viren leads the 10,000 metres from Brendan Foster (364). He won in a world record time of 27 minutes 38.4 seconds, despite having fallen halfway through the race. Viren went on to run the final two laps in 1 minute 56.2 seconds

Viren *factfile*

Born: 22.7.1949, Myrskyla
Country: Finland
Olympic record: 1972: 5,000m gold, 10,000m gold. 1976: 5,000m gold, 10,000m gold, marathon fifth. 1980: 10,000m fifth

The crushing of Coe
Moscow 1980

The disruption of the Montreal Games caused by the boycott by African nations paled into insignificance compared with the boycott that the Moscow Games faced. A year earlier, Soviet troops had gone into Afghanistan. Global condemnation followed, led by the United States, who decided not to send athletes to the Moscow Olympics. Other countries followed suit, leaving just 80 competing nations, compared with 122 eight years earlier.

However, the boycott could have no bearing on the confrontation that track and field supporters everywhere were longing to witness – that between the two British middle-distance runners Steve Ovett and Sebastian Coe. Going into the Games, Coe held the 800 metres world record and shared the 1500 metres world record with Ovett. The two of them had not competed against each other for two years and the unanswered question remained: who was the fastest?

They were both expected to win a gold medal each in their specialised events, Coe in the 800 metres and Ovett in the 1500 metres. The 800 metres came first and both athletes had qualified easily for the final. World record-holder Coe was the favourite as the two great runners finally came head to head. After the first lap the two were perfectly placed when Coe seemed to lose concentration for a second and Ovett made his move. The break was decisive and Ovett went on to take the gold medal by half a second. It was "advantage Ovett" with his preferred distance still to come.

British runner Steve Ovett signals his surprise victory in the 800 metres

MOSCOW 1980   55

Ovett *factfile*

Born: 1955
Country: England
Olympic record: 1976: 800m fifth
1980: 800m gold, 1500m bronze

Coe's comeback

Moscow 1980

"Seb was a worthy winner. I couldn't lift myself after the 800."
Steve Ovett

beaten for more than three years. And after his great victory in the 800 metres a couple of days earlier, he was considered the hot favourite.

The race turned out to be a great tactical success for Coe. He tracked the front runners all the way, including Ovett, right up to the final bend where he lengthened his stride and kicked for home. Ovett didn't have an answer to Coe's final sprint to the tape and could finish only third. Seb Coe's face as he passed the finishing line told its own story. There was simply no way he was going to lose for a second time in a few days.

Above: Triumph followed by exhaustion in the 1,500 metres

Sebastian Coe was inconsolable for a full day after his defeat by arch-rival Steve Ovett in the 800 metres. It now seemed possible that Coe would return home to Britain without a gold medal despite being widely regarded as the best middle-distance runner of the time. The remaining race was the 1500 metres, a distance at which Steve Ovett had not been

Coe *factfile*

Born: 29.9.1956
Country: England
Olympic record: 1980: 1500m gold, 800m silver.
1984: 1500m gold, 800m silver

56

Stevenson rockets to fame
Moscow 1980

Stevenson *factfile*

Born: 1952
Country: Cuba
Olympic record: 1972: boxing heavyweight gold
1976: boxing heavyweight gold
1980: boxing heavyweight gold

After victories for three great American heavyweight boxing champions between 1960 and 1968, the next three titles were to go to a great Cuban boxer. When Teofilo Stevenson beat Pjotr Zayev of the Soviet Union in the 1980 Olympic heavyweight boxing final, the Americans couldn't argue that if their boxers had been there he wouldn't have won. After all, Stevenson had won the heavyweight gold medal at the previous two Olympics when the Americans were taking part. His first victory in Germany against Romanian Ion Alexe would usually have signalled the start of a lucrative professional career. However, the tough Cuban decided to remain an amateur in an attempt to retain his Olympic crown. In 1976 in Montreal, his decision was justified with a victory over another Romanian, Mircea Simon. Again he declined professional offers, to the dismay of Olympic hopefuls all over the world. His hat-trick of golds in Moscow was

Above: Hard-hitting Teofilo Stevenson wins his third heavyweight boxing title at Moscow, equalling the Olympic record of Lazlo Papp of Hungary

the first time this feat had been achieved by a heavyweight boxer and one which many experts feel is unlikely to be surpassed.

Daley's dream debut
Moscow 1980

The Americans had traditionally dominated the decathlon at the Olympics. They had won 10 of the 14 contested, so with their absence the scene was set for someone to make a name for himself. That someone was a charismatic young British athlete by the name of Daley Thompson.

The 21-year-old Thompson went to Moscow relatively unknown – but he took the Games by storm and became a firm favourite with fans thanks to his youthful cockiness and confident smile.

The big threat came from the Russians, Yuriy Kutsenko and Sergey Zhelanov never being far behind. But Thompson held on.

His winning total of 8495, however, was 122 points less than the winning score of the American Bruce Jenner at the previous Olympics. This led to claims from the boycotting nations of a false result. In particular, the West Germans insisted that Jurgen Hingsen would have got the better of Daley. Thompson would have to wait impatiently for four years for the chance to prove them wrong.

Giving it his best shot: Daley Thompson goes all out to win the gold at Moscow

Moscow 1980 *medals*

The top competitors in Moscow were:

			Gold	Silver	Bronze
1. Alexander Ditiatin	(USSR)	Gymnastics	3	4	1
2. Caren Metschuk	(GDR)	Swimming	3	1	–
3. Barbara Krause	(GDR)	Swimming	3	–	–
Rica Reinisch	(GDR)	Swimming	3	–	–
Vladimir Salnikov	(USSR)	Swimming	3	–	–
Vladimir Parfenovich	(USSR)	Canoeing	3	–	–

58

Wells has the will

Moscow 1980

With 65 countries boycotting the 1980 Moscow Games, the Soviets and the East Germans were taking most of the medals. But in the men's track and field events they weren't having it all their own way. Britain was enjoying one of its better Olympics in this department, one athlete in particular setting the pace.

Scottish sprinter Allan Wells went to Moscow intending to win a sprint double, something no other Briton had achieved. In

---

The gold medal-winning time of Allan Wells in 1980 of 10.25 seconds was the slowest winning time since Robert Morrow's 10.50 in 1956.

---

the 100 metres he beat Cuban Silvio Leonard in a photo-finish, both sprinters being timed at 10.25 seconds. Wells's attempt at a sprint double was on.

In the 200 metres, he led the race going into the final few yards but the fast-finishing Italian Pietro Mennea was rapidly catching up. The Italian took the tape with Wells just two hundredths of a second behind.

You shall not pass: Allan Wells was determined to win the 100 metres gold at Moscow. In this heat, he puts Jamaica's Donald Quarrie and Poland's Krzysztof Zwolinski in their place

Wells *factfile*

Born: 1952
Country: Scotland
Olympic record: 1980: 100m gold, 200m silver

Fairytale on ice
Sarajevo 1984

60 The Sarajevo Winter Olympics were to see the rise in popularity of ice dancing as a sport. This was due to two skaters from Nottingham whose skill illuminated the whole of the Games and left one of the most enduring sporting memories of all time in their wake.

Jane Torvill and Christopher Dean had been skating together for nine years before they took ice dancing to another level on February 14, 1984 with their stunning performance in Sarajevo. Their perfectly skated and beautifully choreographed routine to the sound of Ravel's Bolero was watched by a capacity crowd and millions more on television. Everybody knew that they

Torvill & Dean *factfile*

Jayne Torvill Born: 7.10.1957, Nottingham
Christopher Dean Born: 27.7.1958, Nottingham
Country: England
Olympic record: 1980: ice dance fifth
1984: ice dance gold. 1994: ice dance bronze

Hoppe hurtles to triumph
Sarajevo 1984

The sixes on the scoreboard, far left, and the congratulatory flowers, above, mean that Torvill and Dean, left, have hit gold

The 1984 Winter Olympic Games were awarded to Sarajevo in 1978 and at that time no one could have foreseen the troubles that the province would endure just a decade later. This was especially true after the world witnessed the city pull together to put on a spectacular competition.

One of the most exciting events at the Winter Olympics is the bobsleigh. This was to be dominated by the East Germans in Sarajevo and saw the great German bobsleigh driver Wolfgang Hoppe take his first gold medals.

Hoppe is regarded as the greatest bobsleigh driver of all time. With the bobsleigh hurtling down a mile-long course of ice at 90mph it is a role that demands strength, skill and a lot of courage.

Hoppe went on to take gold in the four-man and two-man bobsleigh competitions in Sarajevo to confirm his status as the sport's premier driver.

had seen something special. The judges agreed, awarding a perfect score of nine sixes for artistic interpretation, the first time this had ever been achieved. In taking the gold medal, the skaters went on to receive 12 out of a possible 18 sixes.

Their graceful performance not only popularised the sport but also changed it forever by setting new standards – the true mark of brilliance.

After the Games Torvill and Dean defended their world crown before embarking on a lucrative professional career. But it is their performance in the Olympics that will live on. Those who saw it will never forget where they were on St Valentines Day, 1984.

Hoppe *factfile*

Born: 14.11.1957, Apolda
Country: Germany
Olympic record: 1984: two-man bobsleigh gold, four-man bobsleigh gold. 1988: two-man bobsleigh silver, four-man bobsleigh silver. 1992: four-man bobsleigh silver. 1994: four-man bobsleigh bronze

61

Fast-track: Bobsleigh driver Wolfgang Hoppe hurtled down avenues of ice at 90mph to win his gold medals at Sarajevo

The Budd-Decker disaster
Los Angeles 1984

Mary Decker is supported by her husband Richard Slaney, after her clash with Zola Budd (wearing 151)

Budd and Decker *factfile*

Name: Zola Budd
Born: May 26, 1966, Bloemfontein, SA
Honours: Broke world 5,000 metres record by six seconds in 1984. Appeared in 1992 Olympics for her native South Africa but was eliminated during the heats of the 3,000 metres.

Name: Mary Decker Slaney
Born: February 2, 1958
Honours: Became the youngest US international runner at the age of 14. Held national or world records for events ranging from 800m to 10km during 1983/4.

Eastern Bloc countries boycotted the 1984 Games in Los Angeles. But that is not the controversy for which they will be remembered. It is the women's 3000 metres which pitted all-American golden girl Mary Decker against 17-year-old South African Zola Budd who only qualified for the Olympics by hastily arranging British citizenship. With three laps to go, Budd was leading the race, Decker poised right behind her. The American made her move but hit the trailing leg of bare-footed Budd and was left strewn at the side of the track in tears, her Olympic dream in tatters. Budd stayed on her feet but was cut by Decker's spikes and shaken by the boos of the partisan crowd. She came seventh.

TV replays failed to support Decker camp claims that their girl was deliberately tripped.

Lewis *factfile*

Born: 1.7.1961 **Country:** USA
Olympic record: 1984: 100m gold,
200m gold, 4x100m relay gold,
long jump gold. 1988: 100m gold,
long jump gold, 200m silver.
1992: 4x100m gold, long jump gold.
1996: long jump gold

"Scientists have proven that it's impossible to long-jump 30 feet, but I don't listen to that kind of talk. Thoughts like that have a way of sinking into your feet."
Carl Lewis
(the record is 29ft 4 inches)

63

The greatest of all?

Los Angeles 1984

Games of the XXIIIrd Olympiad Los Angeles 1984

The master: Carl Lewis, above, at full stretch in the 1984 Olympics. In these Games, he was simply unstoppable

At the age of 12, Frederic Carlton Lewis was taken by his father to meet the great Jesse Owens. No one knew at the time that the young Lewis would go on to emulate the feat of Owens by winning four track and field gold medals at one Games. Lewis's victories also came in the same events, the 100 metres, 200 metres, the long-jump and the 4x100 metres relay. All his victories were won with relative ease. He ran the 100 metres in less than 10 seconds and the 200 metres in 19.80 to equal the Olympic record. In truth, the 4x100 metres relay team was probably strong enough to have won without him, but to see him on the anchor leg must have destroyed any hope that the opposition had. The US won by a second from Jamaica.

But Lewis's most impressive victory came in the long-jump where he beat Australian Gary Honey by one foot. He went on to dominate the long-jump for 12 years, as well as winning more gold medals in the sprints, as if to prove that Los Angeles was no fluke and that he could not have been stopped by anyone from the nations that boycotted the Games. The truth is that for two weeks in the summer of 1984, Carl Lewis was an unbeatable winning machine.

It's Daley's day
Los Angeles 1984

Daley on his way to decathlon gold, and letting his shirt do the talking

One of the most eagerly awaited contests at the Los Angeles Olympics was the decathlon. Daley Thompson, the Olympic and world champion, was up against world record holder Jurgen Hingsen. Hingsen had not competed in the previous Olympics but had lost out to Thompson in the 1983 World Championships. Thompson was unable, however, to break Hingsen's world record. The scene was set for a classic confrontation.

The British athlete excelled in the sprint events and so took an early lead in the 100 metres. With the long jump, high jump, shot and 400 metres making up the rest of the day's events, it was Thompson who took an overnight lead. The second day, however, was the big West German's favoured day, with the 110 metres hurdles, discus, pole vault, javelin and 1500 metres to come. Thompson was equal to the challenge and in the last event, the gruelling 1500 metres, he crossed the line with a broad smile knowing he had done more than enough to retain his title – and set a new world record of 8847 points.

The Olympic Games were to end, however, in controversy for the great athlete. First, he upset the host nation by wearing a T-shirt cheekily proclaiming the superstar Carl Lewis to be only the second greatest athlete on earth. Outside America, many thought Daley had a valid point...

Thompson then upset some traditionalists back home in Britain by casually whistling along to the National Anthem while on the winner's podium. All this, however, failed to stop Daley Thompson being hailed as one of the greatest-ever athletes and, in the eyes of many experts, Britain's greatest Olympian.

Thompson *factfile*

Born: 30.7.1958
Country: England
Olympic record:
1980: decathlon gold
1984: decathlon gold
1988: decathlon fourth

Tessa makes her point
Los Angeles 1984

Maybe because she knew that was her best on the day, Lillak retired from the competition after that round. Whitbread, who had looked good coming into the Olympics, was now the only threat to Sanderson.

The leader had to sit and watch as Whitbread persevered – but no matter how hard she tried she couldn't beat her fourth attempt of 67.14 metres, which was only good enough for third place.

Amid joyous scenes, Tessa Sanderson realised that her dream of Olympic gold had just come true.

Sanderson competed in six Olympic Games altogether, which is a record for a British athlete. Fourth place in Barcelona was her next best result after Los Angeles.

65

One of the most nail-biting events at the LA Games was the women's javelin, with three athletes battling for supremacy right to the end. Britain had never come close to winning a women's javelin event but in Tessa Sanderson and Fatima Whitbread the country now boasted two world-class javelin-throwers. The Finns also had a world-class performer in Tiina Lillak and it was these three that contested the gold medal.

In the final, Sanderson threw down the gauntlet with a brilliant first throw of 69.56 metres, which was a new Olympic record. Tiina Lillak then came close to this with her second throw of 69 metres. It was good enough to beat the old world record but not the new one.

Letting go: Tessa Sanderson gives her all and is rewarded with gold, left. Fatima Whitbread, above, shares her delight

Sanderson *factfile*

Born: 1956
Country: England
Olympic record: 1976: javelin tenth.
1984: javelin gold. 1992: javelin fourth

66

Seb's swansong
Los Angeles 1984

"World records are only borrowed."
Seb Coe

The Brits are coming: Sebastian Coe leads Steve Cram and Steve Ovett into the final lap of the 1500 metres at Los Angeles. He followed his triumph by wrapping himself in the Union flag, left, and savoured the victory by showing who was number one, right

After his success in Moscow over 1500 metres, Seb Coe was looking to add the 800 metres gold to his collection in Los Angeles. These Olympics came, however, after a period of two years where Coe rarely competed due to illness or injury.

There was another British challenger to his crown this time. As well as his old adversary, Steve Ovett, a young pretender by the name of Steve Cram had entered the arena. The 800 metres was again to end in disappointment as Coe had to settle for another silver medal.

The defeat was not to one of his compatriots, however, as the Brazilian Joaquim Cruz took the gold medal and broke the Olympic record in the process. The 1500 metres was a different story and the British runners were in control from beginning to end.

Seb Coe managed to hold off the challenge of Steve Cram to repeat his medal count of four years earlier with one gold and one silver. Cram finished second and Ovett fourth as the British continued to dominate the middle-distance events, with Seb Coe leading the way.

When sport met showbiz
Los Angeles 1984

One of the greatest things about the Olympics is the diversity of sports it brings together. From archery to yachting, there is a sport that appeals to everyone. At the LA Games there were a total of 221 events in 21 different sports. This was more than at any other Olympics in the past.

One of the events to make its debut at the Games was synchronised swimming. Not surprisingly, the Americans dominated this event with one person in particular benefiting from its introduction into the Olympics. Tracie Ruiz, along with her partner Candy Costie, won the first gold medals in this event in the duet discipline.

A day later, Ruiz went on to win her second gold medal with a victory over the Canadian Carolyn Waldo in the single event.

The sport proved popular, to the surprise of some observers. But there were large crowds at the swimming arena and the event was here to stay. Tracie Ruiz went on to perform in the Seoul Olympics, where Carolyn Waldo reversed the result of four years earlier and beat Ruiz into second place.

Left: Tracie and Candy on display at the poolside

Majestic Moses
Los Angeles 1984

Ed Moses had a point to prove at the Los Angeles Olympics, namely that he was the world's best 400 metres hurdler. He did it, left, without having to stretch to his limits

68

The men's 400 metres hurdles at the Los Angeles Olympics was probably the easiest result to predict out of all the events. Since 1977, Ed Moses had remained unbeaten and on his 28th birthday the previous year had again broken the world record with a time of 47.02 seconds.

Moses had exploded onto the world scene at the Montreal Olympics with a world record-breaking victory to take the gold medal. A year later he lost to West Germany's Harald Schmid but didn't lose another race for a decade. The US boycott stopped Moses competing in Moscow, where East Germany's Volker Beck won in 48.7 seconds, more than a second slower than Moses' time in Montreal. This left the US athlete with a point to prove on his home soil. The majestic Moses never looked in any trouble during the final and took the gold without seemingly going flat out. Harald Schmid finished third and the American Danny Harris took the silver medal.

Three years later, with Moses approaching 32, Harris finally brought the maestro's amazing run of 122 victories to an end.

Moses *factfile*

Born: 31.8.1955, Dayton, Ohio
Country: USA
Olympic record:
1976: 400m hurdles gold
1984: 400m hurdles gold
1988: 400m hurdles bronze

Carmen scores for golden Katarina

Calgary 1988

"It's hard to skate last. It can show you are only human. Anybody can make mistakes."

Katarina Witt

The figure skating duel between the two best female skaters in the world, Katarina Witt of East Germany and Debi Thomas of the United States, attracted a TV audience averaging 43 million. It was the highest ever in Winter Olympic Games history.

What they saw was a tense, pressure-filled skating rink which inspired one skater – Witt – to great heights, and caused the other – Thomas – to crumble.

Witt skated before Thomas in the final freestyle section and her balletic interpretation of Carmen earned her the chance to become the first female skater to defend an Olympic title since Sonja Henie had won in 1928, 1932 and 1936. But there was a real chance Thomas could overtake her. Before Thomas took to the ice, Canadian Elizabeth Manley skated the routine of her life to beat Witt in the freestyle programme (the first skater to do so in five years) and put her in the overall silver medal berth behind the East German.

Debi Thomas took to the ice as the last skater but the pressure proved too much and her routine was awry. She landed poorly on her first jump and from then on her heart wasn't in the performance. Witt once more took the gold.

Skating it: Katarina Witt in action at Calgary on her way to winning the women's figure-skating gold.
Far left: Acknowledging her richly deserved applause

Witt *factfile*

Born: 3.12.1965
Country: East Germany
Olympic record: 1984: figure skating gold. 1988: figure skating gold
1994: figure skating seventh

Eddie the Eagle flops to fame
Calgary 1988

He was an unexpected hero of the Great Britain team for the 1988 Winter Olympics, and living proof that this country often loves a loser more than a winner. At first glance, you wouldn't pick Eddie Edwards, dubbed rather cruelly "The Eagle", for a ski jumper. And that's because he wasn't. But he tried hard.

Edwards, a plasterer from Cheltenham, jumped, or rather fell, his way into the record books by competing in two ski jump events in the 1988 Games. He finished 58th in the 70-metre jump and 55th in the 90-metre event. Dead last in each.

But the small, bespectacled Eagle was a cult hero and when he returned home he was given the sort of paparazzi reception that pop stars receive. And why not? As Edwards pointed out, he was an Olympic competitor and Britain's ski jump record-holder –

"I know I'm just Eddie Edwards the plasterer, and sport is so professional now. But haven't I brought something back to Olympic sport? Like, what did they used to call it? Ah, yes. Taking part."
Eddie Edwards

although, admittedly, he was also Britain's only ski jumper. But through adversity comes strength, or in Eddie's case, a few quid. From his antics at Calgary, The Eagle landed a nice nest egg from the media circus, appeared on the Terry Wogan show and even recorded a single.

The Eagle is landing – Eddie at Calgary in the 70 metres hill final

Marksmen bang on target
Seoul 1988

strong favourites to battle it out for gold in South Korea.

This event is mentally very demanding, requiring immense concentration. Competitors must shoot from three different positions – prone, kneeling and standing – for the ultimate test of precision.

Malcolm Cooper once again passed the test with flying colours as he amassed 1279.3 points. Allan improved on his bronze medal, taking the silver with 1275.6 points. This victory was a personal triumph for the talented Cooper, who made his own rifle and bullets. He became one of Britain's unsung double Olympic heroes.

Steady, aim... Fired-up Malcolm Cooper is about to make his mark in the small-bore rifle championship

One of the strongest events for Britain at the Seoul Olympics was the three-position small-bore rifle shooting. Traditionally, this is not the world's most popular sport but the power of the Olympics means that even the most obscure disciplines receive their 15 minutes of fame.

The two men who were carrying British hopes were Malcolm Cooper and Alister Allan. These two sharp-shooters had won the gold and bronze medals respectively at the Los Angeles Games and were

Cooper *factfile*

Born: 20.12.1947 Camberley, Surrey
Country: England
Olympic record:
1984: small-bore rifle (3 position) gold
1988: small-bore rifle (3 position) gold

Jolly hockey sticks — it's gold for Britain

Seoul 1988

Sixty-eight years after the team had last collected an Olympic Gold medal in this event, the hockey players of Great Britain were once again crowned as Olympic champions following a 3-1 victory over West Germany in the final.

Britain's previous successes in Olympic hockey came in the 1908 London Games and then at Antwerp in 1920. Four years before Seoul, Britain had enjoyed a successful campaign to collect the bronze medal but now, with the powerful team from Pakistan (defending champions from 1984) surprisingly eliminated at an early stage, the door was open for Britain to better its Los Angeles bronze.

A superb 3-2 win over Australia in the semi-finals set up the clash with West Germany in the final. Forward Sean Kerly was the hero of the semi, grabbing all three goals for Britain, the winning effort just four minutes from time.

In the final, Imran Sherwani ensured that Britain would not only avenge a preliminary group game defeat against the Germans, but also that the gold medals would be heading for British shores.

Sherwani scored twice from open play, and with Sean Kerly adding another from a penalty corner, Britain had a 3-0 lead after 53 minutes. Despite many attempts on goal, the Germans breached Britain's heroic defence only once and had to settle for their third silver medal in men's Olympic hockey.

72

Stephen Batchelor celebrates England's third goal in their 3-1 victory over West Germany, though Sean Kerly was later credited as the scorer. Two-goal hero Imran Sherwani is in the background

Seoul 1988 *factfile*

Tournament records:

Top scorers in the 1988 men's hockey:

9 Floris Jan Bove Lander (Netherlands)

8 Mark Hager (Australia)

8 Sean Kerly (Great Britain)

There were no red cards shown throughout the men's tournament. Netherlands and Canada each amassed 13 green cards and Kenya topped the yellow cards with six.

Lewis and Bowe begin their feud
Seoul 1988

ennox Lewis, a 23-year-old English-born boxer who had lived in Canada for 16 years and chose to represent them as an Olympic competitor, rewarded his adopted country with its first boxing gold medal for 56 years.

Lewis beat the USA's Riddick Bowe to the super-heavyweight crown, stopping the American in the second round. Earlier that day, the competition had been marred by the controversial award of a gold medal to one of the host country's fighters. The loser was an American, Roy Jones, so the US team weren't best pleased when Lewis rubbed salt in the wounds by mauling one of their favoured fighters.

To celebrate bringing home a rare gold, Lewis was given a ticker-tape welcome in his adopted hometown of Kitchener in southern Ontario.

Although Bowe and Lewis never fought again, they would spend years engaged in a war of words – with Lewis having the last laugh by becoming undisputed world champion at the turn of the Millennium.

Left: Lennox on parade in the Seoul Olympics closing ceremony and, above, sending Riddick Bowe to defeat in the heavyweight final

Lewis *factfile*

Born: 2.9.1965, London, England
Country: Canada
Olympic record:
1988: boxing super-heavyweight gold

Bubka proves he's the master

Seoul 1988

Sergei Bubka was a man due for an Olympic gold medal, missing out as he did on the opportunity to compete in the 1984 Los Angeles Games because of the Soviet Union boycott. Bubka had literally launched himself to prominence in the pole-vault in 1983 when, at the World Championships, he secured gold by clearing 18 feet eight-and-a-quarter inches with his first attempt.

Two weeks before the LA Games, Bubka, the world record-holder, vaulted six inches higher than the Olympic gold medallist would achieve, but politics denied him the chance for gold.

Not so in Seoul where Bubka led a Soviet clean sweep in the pole-vault. Bubka cleared 19 feet four and a quarter inches to take first place. He toyed with the idea of trying to break the magical 20-feet barrier but decided to save that for another day (he finally did it in 1991). A gold medal, even if it did arrive four years late, was enough for the time being.

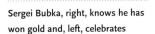

Bubka *factfile*

Born: 1964, Voroshilovgrad, Ukraine
Country: Russia
Olympic record: 1988: pole vault gold

Sergei Bubka, right, knows he has won gold and, left, celebrates

From hero to zero in 9.79 seconds

Seoul 1988

75

> *"They can always take back the medal, but they can't take away my speed. I had been training for 13 years, for my life, for this one moment and it just disappeared like that, in a second."*
> Ben Johnson

It should have been the race of all time – the fastest men on Earth going head to head for the greatest Olympic prize of all, the men's 100 metres gold. It ended up as the biggest scandal in Olympic history.

The finishing order was Ben Johnson (Canada), Carl Lewis (USA), Linford Christie (Great Britain). All three broke 10 seconds and at the time it was a fantastic race.

But just 72 hours later the memories were shattered by the revelation that Johnson had tested positive for Stanazolol – a banned anabolic steroid – in a routine drug test. He was stripped of his gold medal and suspended from competition for two years. Johnson denied taking steroids, claiming that, apart from cortisone shots to ease a heel injury, the only medication he knowingly took was an energy-enhancing drink mix of sarsaparilla and ginseng.

The gold medal was awarded instead to Carl Lewis.

Johnson *factfile*

Born: 1961 **Country:** USA
Broke 10 seconds in the 100 metres on nine occasions. Winner of 23 prestigious awards for athletic achievement. Reinstated after two-year ban in September 1990.

Dash for gold: Ben Johnson leads the field ahead of Carl Lewis, Linford Christie and the rest of the world's greats to win an astonishing 100 metres victory at the Seoul Olympics. His triumph was to turn to disqualification and disgrace

Greg Louganis arrived at Seoul as the defending Olympic champion having won the 1984 Olympic springboard event by the biggest margin in the history of the Games. He had then won the platform diving event as well in a performance ranked as the greatest ever by a diver and one that was unlikely to be equalled.

But Louganis knew at Seoul that he was infected with the HIV virus, a secret he wouldn't reveal until years after retiring. In qualifying for the springboard competition, on his ninth dive, Louganis misjudged his

> *"You couldn't have written a better script. That was the biggest dive of his career."*
>
> Ron O'Brien, coach to Greg Louganis

76

Greg's 'dive of death'
Seoul 1988

leap and as he went into a reverse somersault, his head caught the board, causing a terrible gash. He was shaken but was back on the board half an hour later to continue his qualifying dives, which fortunately didn't count to the final marks. He qualified, and then went on to win the springboard event.

In the platform event, Louganis trailed Xiong of China with just his final dive to come. He chose what had become dubbed "the Dive of Death" – a highly difficult dive so called because five years earlier Sergei Chalibashvili of the Soviet Union had attempted it and struck his head on the concrete platform on the way down and had plunged to his death. Louganis was among the competitors that day and had witnessed the tragedy.

So with that in his memory, and a patch covering his own head-wound from a few days before, Louganis prepared to win his second gold medal of the Games and repeat the double of four years earlier. His last dive in Olympic competition had to be near perfect to win. And it was. He scored 86.70 to beat Xiong by just 1.14 points.

Agonisingly close: Louganis misjudges his dive and his head hits the board

Louganis *factfile*

Born: 29.1.1960
Country: USA
Olympic record:
1976: highboard silver, springboard sixth.
1984: highboard gold, springboard gold.
1988: highboard gold, springboard gold

Flo-Jo paints the town red
Seoul 1988

"It was a 20-year dream. At that moment I knew everything was worth it. I felt so happy inside that I had won it I just had to let it out."

Flo-Jo on crossing the 100 metres winning line

After winning a silver medal in the 200 metres in 1984, Florence Griffith-Joyner had virtually retired. However, she returned in 1987 to take silver at the World Championships – and in 1988 she relaunched herself as a dazzling sprint talent. Not only could she run like the wind, she was sexy with it. She announced her speedy intentions with a 100 metres record of 10.49 seconds in the US Olympic trials, clad in a figure-hugging one-piece body suit.

Flo-Jo wasn't allowed to wear the body suit for the Olympics proper, but she still caught the eye with her long nails gaudily painted in patriotic colours. And, of course, with her speed.

That speed propelled Flo-Jo to a Seoul Games haul of four medals crowned by the 100 metres.

En route to that gold medal she broke the Olympic record in the qualifying rounds by setting a mark of 10.88 seconds. In the quarter-finals she then lowered the new mark to 10.62. In the semi-final she was drawn against her East German rival for gold, Heike Dreschler, who ran a lifetime best of 10.91 seconds. It wasn't good enough. She trailed Flo-Jo by two metres.

A good start in the final eased her into the lead and by 70 metres the race was as good as over. With 10 metres left, the smile was dazzling, and the arms were in the air well before the finishing line. It all took just 10.54 seconds.

Flo-Jo left Seoul with 100 metres, 200 metres and 4 x 100 metres golds, and silver in the 4 x 400. Her success was astonishing, but sadly short-lived. She retired at the age of 29, had a baby and began training for the marathon – but died of a brain tumour in 1998.

Flo-Jo shows off her medals – and her fingernails!

Griffith-Joyner *factfile*

Born: 21.12.1959, Los Angeles, Cal
Died: 21.9.1998 **Country:** USA
Olympic record: 1984: 200m silver
1988: 100m gold, 200m gold, 4x100m relay gold, 4x400m relay silver

Otto finally makes her mark
Seoul 1988

If she had been allowed to compete in the 1984 Los Angeles Games, East German swimmer Kristin Otto might have rewritten the history books a little earlier than she finally did. Otto was voted the world's best female swimmer in 1984, but didn't get the chance to prove it. But four years later she underlined her credentials.

Her success in the pool was unprecedented and a real blow to the

> *"I wanted to win a gold medal,*
> *but I never dreamed of six."*
> Kristin Otto

Americans, who had enjoyed things very much their own way four years previously.

By winning the 50 metres freestyle on the first occasion the distance was ever raced by women at the Olympics, Otto secured her sixth gold medal of the Games – the first woman to achieve such a feat. It beat the previous record haul by a woman of four golds, by Kornelia Ender in 1976. Only Mark Spitz had ever done better than Otto in a single Games, and that by one more gold.

The blonde, six-foot, 22-year-old Otto won the 100 metres freestyle, 100 metres butterfly, 100 metres backstroke, 400 metres freestyle relay, 400 metres medley relay and 50 metres freestyle. This haul meant she had captured exactly half of her country's 12 gold medals in the Seoul pool. The sixth gold came as a bit of a surprise to Otto because she thought she was weak in that event. She thought that her winning time of 25.5 seconds should not have been fast enough to win. But it was.

Above: Kristin swimming for gold

Otto *factfile*

Born: 7.2.1965, Leipzig
Country: East Germany
Olympic record:
1988: 50m freestyle gold, 100m freestyle gold, 100m backstroke gold, 100m butterfly gold, 4x100m freestyle relay gold, 4x100m medley relay gold

78

79

Graf *factfile*

Born: 14.6.1969
Country: Germany
Olympic record:
1988: singles gold, doubles bronze.
1992: singles silver

Match point: Steffi serves for gold and, below, celebrates her triumph

Steffi's golden slam
Seoul 1988

Having achieved the tennis Grand Slam of winning Wimbledon, the US Open, the French Open and the Australian Open in the same calendar year – 19-year-old tennis wonder-girl Steffi Graf turned to the Olympic Games.

Tiredness was not a factor and there was never any thought of taking the easy way out. That was not in the German's mind. Not then, not ever. Graf wanted to become the first player, male or female, to achieve the Golden Slam – all four of the tennis major titles and an Olympic gold medal. And as 1988 was the first time tennis had been an Olympic medal sport for 64 years, the timing could not have been

better. Facing her in the Olympic final was 18-year-old Argentinian Gabriela Sabatini, who had beaten Graf twice in competition earlier in the year. She gave Graf a run for her money in the early stages, but squandered break points and made mistakes at vital times as Graf's groundstrokes began to overwhelm her.

In the end, the winning margin of 6-3, 6-3 was a comfortable one, Graf admitting that her strength was staying at the baseline and wearing Sabatini down by making her run around the court .

The Argentinian's lack of stamina was a weakness that Graf thought she could take advantage of, and so it proved. The win was her 40th consecutive victory of the year, during which time she had won, in total, 66 times and lost just twice. It was a year to remember.

Biondi the bionic swimmer

Seoul 1988

American swimmer Matt Biondi equalled the great Mark Spitz by winning seven medals in one Games, but the seven for Spitz were all gold. Biondi managed five golds, a silver and a bronze.

Biondi shrank away from suggestions before the Games that he could equal Spitz's seven-gold tally. At the end of the competition he was surprised he managed five. Three came from relay teams but as an individual he claimed the 50 metres and 100 metres freestyle golds, came second in the 100 metres butterfly and third in the 200 metres freestyle.

The fifth and final gold for Biondi came in the last event of the swimming competition: the 400 metres medley relay.

The US team swam superbly to win by five metres in a world record time of 3:36.93, shattering the previous best record by one and a half seconds. Biondi had played a role in that record, too, anchoring the 1985 team with the freestyle leg.

But Biondi then figured that

Victory wave: Matt Biondi celebrates winning gold in the 50 metres

> *"Winning seven medals feels great. But it's over. I've always swum because I had goals out there. I don't have any goals left."*
> Matt Biondi

he couldn't get any better than his achievements in Seoul and announced his intention, at 22, to retire. He did, however, go on to compete in the 1992 Games.

Biondi *factfile*

Born: 6.10.1965
Country: USA
Olympic record:
1984: 4 x 100m freestyle relay gold.
1988: 50m freestyle gold, 100m freestyle gold, 4 x 100m freestyle relay gold, 4 x 100m medley relay gold, 4 x 200m freestyle relay gold, 100m butterfly silver, 200m freestyle bronze.
1992: 4 x 100m freestyle relay gold, 4 x 100m medley relay gold, 50m freestyle silver, 100m freestyle fifth

80

81

Tomba 'La Bomba'
Albertville 1992

Alberto Tomba was already a superhero in his native Italy by the time he lined up to compete in the men's slalom skiing events in Albertville, France, in 1992. Four years earlier, the playboy skier had put in a double-gold medal performance at the Calgary Winter Games in the slalom and giant slalom. And in 1992 he had won seven World Cup events.

Tomba took the lead after the first run of the giant slalom, with 0.13 seconds to spare on Marc Girardelli. The final competitor to take to the slopes on the second run, Tomba was without parallel and increased his lead to a winning margin of 0.19 seconds. The first

leg of the double in what had been dubbed the "Alberto-Ville" Games was complete.

But in the slalom, the last Alpine event of the Games, Tomba started dreadfully and could only manage to place 1.58 seconds behind the leader in sixth place. Tomba knew the second run had to be special. And it was. He gained split seconds at each gate, dancing his way down the course. He crossed the line in 1:44.67 to a roar that might have carried to

his home town of Bologna. All he could do was wait.

Each racer to follow had led Tomba after the first run, but none was able to match him after the second. Tomba was in silver medal position with just the first-run leader, Christian Jagge, to go. Jagge skied hard but lost time from his lead all the way down. When he finally crossed the line he had just 0.28 seconds to spare. It was enough for gold.

Left: Tomba in the giant slalom

Tomba *factfile*

Born: 19.12.1966, Bologna
Country: Italy
Olympic record: 1988: giant slalom gold, slalom gold 1992: giant slalom gold, slalom silver. 1994: slalom silver

Jackie jumps for joy

Barcelona 1992

"Jackie is the greatest multi-event athlete ever, man or woman."

Bruce Jenner, 1976 Olympic decathlon champion

Barcelona'92

© 1988 COOB 92, S.A. All rights reserved TM

82

Jackie Joyner-Kersee went to the Barcelona Games full of hope and expectation that she would retain the heptathlon gold that she had won so spectacularly four years earlier in Seoul with a new world record of 7,291 points.

Since she had won heptathlon silver at her first Olympics in 1984, she had rarely been beaten and then only when injured, as at the Tokyo World Championships when she suffered cramp in the 200 metres and fell.

Barcelona had no such drama. Joyner-Kersee started superbly with 12.85 in the 100m hurdles and six feet three-and-a-quarter in the high jump. But a poor shot-putt performance

Above: A l-o-n-g jump before putting the shot

– 46ft four-and-a-quarter when she was hoping to break 50 feet – meant that, for once, Joyner-Kersee had real competition in Germany's Sabine Braun and Irina Belova of the Unified team (the former Soviet Union). But on the second day, Joyner-Kersee stamped her authority in her favourite event, the long jump, of which she was the world champion.

She followed an average first jump with 23 feet three-and-a-half inches – well over the seven metres she and her coach, husband Bob, had aimed for. Her rivals faltered – and with fine performances in the 200 metres, javelin and 800 metres, Joyner-Kersee triumphed again.

Joyner-Kersee *factfile*

Born: 6.3.1962, St Louis, Illinois
Country: USA
Olympic record: 1984: heptathlon silver, long jump fifth. 1988: heptathlon gold, long jump gold
1992: heptathlon gold, long jump bronze
1996: long jump bronze

Boardman *factfile*

Born: 26.8.1968, Hoylake
Country: England
Olympic record: 1992: cycling 4,000m individual pursuit gold
1996: cycling road time trial bronze

Boardman at full speed on that bike

his world title, Boardman, without the Lotus bike, had finished fifth, nine seconds behind his rival.

In the Olympic final, however, Boardman and Lotus reigned

> *"The bike has significant advantages, otherwise I wouldn't be using it."*
> Chris Boardman

Bike to the future

Barcelona 1992

Was it the man or the machine? Or a combination of the two working in perfect harmony and bringing Britain's Chris Boardman such a resounding gold medal in the 4,000 metres cycle pursuit at Barcelona?

A cabinet-maker by trade, Boardman had set his sights on Olympic gold in 1992. The revolutionary Lotus bike design, which reduced wind resistance and drag and therefore increased speed, helped a lot. But he still had to pedal.

Boardman set a world best time of 4 minutes 24.496 seconds in the quarter-finals. The following day he zipped through the semi, earning the right to meet reigning world champion Jens Lehmann of Germany.

A year earlier, when Lehmann had won

supreme. The riders start 250 metres apart on opposite sides of the track, but Boardman was so fast that he did something that had rarely happened before, certainly not in an Olympic final – he caught Lehmann with a lap to spare.

Boardman had said before the Games that he thought the new bike might make the difference between fourth place and a gold medal. He was right.

After the race, his rival, Lehmann, was magnanimous. He said: "My defeat had nothing to do with Boardman's machine. Simply, I lost because of the performance of the man I met in the final."

The Essex girl with real class

Barcelona 1992

Twenty-six-year-old Sally Gunnell, who learned to run the hurdles by jumping straw bales on her father's Essex chicken farm, had a dual responsibility at Barcelona. She was the women's team captain and a good prospect for the 400 metres hurdles gold.

The men's team captain, Linford Christie, had already led by example, winning the 100 metres gold. It was only right that Gunnell should follow suit.

Second place in the previous year's World Championships had given Gunnell the belief that she was good enough and things fell into place as she reached the seventh hurdle of the final, fractionally behind leader Sandra Farmer-Patrick, the US favourite. But Farmer-Patrick made a hash of that seventh hurdle, and Gunnell landed in the lead.

Her strong finish pulled her clear of the field and as she crossed the line she was three metres ahead. Her winning time was 53.23 seconds.

Sally Gunnell hurtling towards gold

"It's something you dream about. When you are confronted by reality, it's hard for it to sink in. I'm just trying to retain every moment in my mind. I think I'll be grinning for the rest of my life."
Sally Gunnell

84

Gunnell *factfile*

Born: 29.7.1966
Country: England
Olympic record: 1988: 400m hurdles fifth. 1992: 400m hurdles gold, 4x400m relay bronze

The defining image of the 1992 Barcelona Games was of British sprinter Linford Christie, bug-eyed and focused as he pounded through the 100 metres final to become, at the age of 32, the oldest man to win the sprint gold.

Christie's build-up to Barcelona had gone unbelievably well. He had lost only one 100 metres race that year, and that by

85

> "Apart from Carl Lewis, I think I've got the best second-half surge. So I used it."
> Linford Christie

It's Christie's crown
Barcelona 1992

just one hundredth of a second. But he had been in good form before and still managed to lose – to Carl Lewis and a drug-tainted Ben Johnson at Seoul in 1988. And then in a sublime sprint race in the Tokyo World Championships in 1991, Christie had clocked a European record of 9.92 seconds in the final and still finished, unbelievably,

fourth. Great rival Carl Lewis won in a world record of 9.86, followed by Leroy Burrell in 9.88 and Dennis Mitchell in 9.91. Yet Barcelona belonged to Christie despite the USA's Burrell throwing down the gauntlet and beating the Briton in the semi-final. But 90 minutes later, when it counted for medals, it was Christie who was most composed and Burrell who showed nerves by triggering a false start.

Jamaica's Frankie Fredericks got away best from the blocks, but Christie, a picture of concentration, overhauled him in the second 50 metres and crossed the line as the winner in 9.96 seconds with Fredericks second in 10.02. Burrell languished in fifth place. The old man had the last laugh.

A medal of tarnished gold

Barcelona 1992

Christie *factfile*

Born: 2.4.1965
Country: England
Olympic record: 1988: 100m silver, 4x100m relay silver. 1992: 100m gold 1996: 100m disqualified

Above: Joyful Christie raises his arms in triumph as he crosses the 100 metres line

The final of the men's 10,000 metres should have been decided on the track. Instead, the verdict came from a committee room. With less than a mile to go, 20-year-old Kenyan Richard Chelimo led narrowly from Moroccan Khalid Skah. The two caught up a tail-ender, another Moroccan, Hammou Boutayeb, who should have moved aside to be lapped. But he did not – choosing instead to mix himself up with the two leaders. With a lap to go, Boutayeb dropped out, but by then Skah had gathered to attack and outkicked Chelimo down the final stretch.

The crowd sensed that an injustice had been done, that Boutayeb had deliberately blocked Chelimo to help his team-mate. Both the Moroccans were disqualified.

Then the committee went into action and studied the TV replays. The decision was that Boutayeb had not interfered, at least not with the knowledge and collusion of Skah, who was reinstated as champion 24 hours after the race had been run.

When he stepped up to collect his gold medal, Skah was booed, while Chelimo was loudly cheered. The catcalls continued through the national anthem and even as Skah left the stadium with his prize.

> *"What happened to Chelimo in the 10,000m was unacceptable in any forum. He was cheated out of a gold medal."*
> Steve Nearman, Washington Times

86

Chelimo and reinstated Skah at the medal ceremony

> *"I deserve the medal. I ran in the heats. I ran every lap. I did not ride a scooter, I ran fairly."*
> Khalid Skah

87

Gail Devers tops her remarkable recovery with a famous sprint at Barcelona

Devers back from the brink

Barcelona 1992

The women's 100m final at Barcelona was an epic. It had everything. Top-class sprinters, fast times, a close finish and a human interest story to pluck at the heartstrings.

Firstly the race. Five runners seemed to hit the line at the same time – so close together that even the still-frame photo shown on the stadium big screen couldn't distinguish one placing from another. Russia's Irina Privalova, the USA's Gail Devers and Gwen Torrance, Jamaica's Juliet Cuthbert and ever-competitive Merlene Ottey. All within a whisker of gold.

But the one who was adjudged to have crossed the finish line first is where the human interest comes in. Gail Devers took gold – and less than 18 months before she had been so ill with Graves

"Use me as an example. When the walls are closing in, when someone doesn't know where to turn, tell people I was there. I kept going. So can others. Sounds like a sermon, doesn't it?"

Gail Devers

Disease that she couldn't even walk to the bathroom unaided. A doctor told her that if she had left it another couple of days before seeing him, her feet, which were swollen and smothered in blood blisters, would have required amputation.

At Barcelona those same feet whisked her down the 100m in 10.82 seconds – into a one metre-per-second breeze. Taking that into account, only world record holder Florence Griffith Joyner had run quicker. Talk about a miraculous recovery.

100

Devers *factfile*

Born: 19.11.1966, Seattle
Country: USA
Olympic record:
1992: 100m gold, 100m hurdles fifth.
1996: 100m gold, 4x100m gold,
100m hurdles fourth

Nearly there, son
Barcelona 1992

The semi-final of the 400 metres at Barcelona was British runner Derek Redmond's last race as an official athlete, and his father Jim's first as an unofficial one.

Redmond, who had been forced to withdraw from the 400 metres in Seoul four years earlier because of Achilles tendon trouble, never officially finished his Barcelona semi-final because the record book says his race was abandoned. But Redmond did cross the finishing line, as did his father, who had dashed from the stands when he

---

After the Barcelona Games, Redmond had several operations but was never able to run competitively again. He met swimmer Sharron Davies at Barcelona and subsequently married her.

---

saw his son tear a hamstring after 150 metres, fall, and then get up and continue at a painful hobble towards the line.

Jim Redmond vaulted a concrete barrier so that he could support his son, who at first didn't recognise him and tried to push him away. The two stumbled the final 100 metres together to cross the line. The time was unrecorded but those who witnessed the drama will never forget it.

Father and son received 3,000 letters from all over the world in the aftermath of the Games.

Helping hand: Jim Redmond supports his son to the line

88

"It was just fatherly instinct...
seeing your son in trouble and helping."
Jim Redmond

Skulduggery on ice
Lillehammer 1994

By winning the figure skating ahead of Nancy Kerrigan at Lillehammer, the Ukraine's Oksana Baiul became her country's first gold medal winner.

Nancy Kerrigan (in white) and Tonya Harding ignore each other in pre-competition training. Right: Defeat is unbearable for Tonya

Nancy Kerrigan won the silver medal at the 1994 Games in the women's figure-skating and very nearly the gold. But is was no thanks to her US "team-mate" Tonya Harding. She became implicated in the most bizarre scandal ever to rock the graceful figure-skating scene.

At the US Olympic trials a few months earlier, Nancy Kerrigan, leaving the ice after skating practice, was attacked by a male assailant. The man hit Kerrigan on the right knee with a blunt object and in an instant Kerrigan thought her world had collapsed. Would she be fit to compete at the Games? Ultimately she was.

However, four men were later arrested in connection with the attack, one of them being Harding's ex-husband. They implicated Kerrigan's rival in the plot, and only some legal wrangling allowed Harding to skate – against Kerrigan among others – at the Games.

While Kerrigan skated the performance of her life and won silver behind Oksana Baiul, Harding made a mess of her routine. She cut it short after 30 seconds and tearfully

"I am committed to seeking professional help and turning my full attention to getting my personal life in order. This objective is more important than my skating."
Tonya Harding

asked for another chance, which was given. But in court there was no second chance. Harding avoided jail only by pleading guilty to hindering the investigation into the attack and accepting a long list of penalties.

A new gold medal for Ali

Atlanta 1996

Atlanta 1996
TM © 1992 ACOG

Two people were killed and more than 100 injured in a bomb blast in a park as the Olympic Games at Atlanta, Georgia, got under way. It seemed at first that the Games here would always be remembered for that terrible

Ali, boxing as Cassius Clay in the 1960 Rome Olympics, had won the 178lbs class on a unanimous decision over three-time European champion Zbigniew Pietrzykowski of Poland (full story on page 37).

He went on to become the first man to win the professional world heavyweight championship on three separate occasions.

"I think it was a big slap in the face for boxing... He was a draft dodger. If they'd asked me, hell, I'd have run all the way up there and lit the flame. He's a lot of noise, lot of mouth."

Joe Frazier – old rival but still no friend of Ali

outrage. But Muhammad Ali changed all that. He opened the Games by lighting the Olympic flame with the ceremonial torch. For some, it was a sad sight to see the former loudmouthed but brilliant boxer who had fought, danced and talked his way to stardom cut a very different figure, struggling against Parkinson's disease.

But at half-time in the basketball final, Ali again appeared and IOC President Juan Antonio Samaranch presented him with a gold medal. It was a replacement for the one that Ali, then Cassius Clay, had won in the 1960 Olympics and later thrown into a Kentucky River in a civil rights protest.

Ali, with shaking hands, raised the new gold medal to his lips and kissed it. The crowd chanted his name. It was just like old times.

Muhammad Ali, wearing his new medal, receives congratulations from the US Dream Team who beat Yugoslavia in the 1996 basketball final

90

I'm the strongest man in the world
Atlanta 1996

A ndrey Chemerkin, Russia's super-heavyweight lifter, re-established himself as the globe's strongest man when he broke the world record in the clean-and-jerk final. He did it with some theatre, too, keeping the crowd on their seats to his very last, and ultimately successful, lift. The weight was a massive 573lbs, 11lbs greater than the world record set by Germany's Ronny Weller just a few minutes earlier.

Chemerkin's superhuman effort in the last lift elevated him to a record-equalling total of 1,008 lbs, and ensured that Weller was relegated to silver medal position.

"The German, Weller, had already thrown his shoes into the crowd, so sure was he that he'd won gold. Chemerkin then lifted the greatest poundage ever hoisted by a human being to foil him. Weller fainted clean away with the shock."
Total Sport

Above: Andrey Chemerkin holds 108kg and, left, jumps for joy to celebrate his success

Redgrave rows into the record books
Atlanta 1996

Steve Redgrave had been top of the rowing tree in one class or another since 1984. He won his first gold medal in Los Angeles, added another in 1988 in the coxless pairs with Andrew Holmes, and a third in a row at Barcelona with Matthew Pinsent.

Adding a fourth at Atlanta, again in tandem with Pinsent, would be a record. No rower had achieved it before. Only three other athletes in the history of the Olympics had managed it. Four in a row was a rare feat indeed.

But that was enough to motivate Redgrave, then 33 years old. And sure enough, he and Pinsent were the dominant force of the coxless pairs competition – adding Atlanta gold to their already impressive haul of Barcelona Olympic gold, four consecutive World Championship titles and more than 50 international wins as a team.

Redgrave admitted that the thought of winning four in a row had entered his mind just a matter of days after the 1992 final at Barcelona. What were his thoughts

Redgrave *factfile*

Born: 23.3.1962, Marlow
Country: England
Olympic record:
1984: coxed fours gold
1988: coxless pairs gold, coxed pairs bronze
1992: coxless pairs gold
1996: coxless pairs gold

on the possibility of five in a row at Sydney 2000? "I've had enough. If anyone sees me near a boat again they can shoot me," Redgrave said with his latest gold hung around his neck in Atlanta.

And yet he began training again just weeks later – with no visible signs of bullet wounds.

Pulling power: Steve Redgrave and Matthew Pinsent pull out the stops on their way to gold

He wore gold running shoes to race in, ran in a bizarre, upright style that contradicted all logic – and performed such an awesome feat that it left onlookers wondering if they had just seen the bionic man. But

"When Michael Johnson's running, it's a fact there are two races. At least I won the second race."

400m silver medallist Roger Black

The bionic man?
Atlanta 1996

93

Johnson *factfile*

Born: 13.9.1967, Dallas, Texas
Country: USA
Olympic record: 1992: 4x400m gold
1996: 200m gold, 400m gold

Emotional tears as Johnson receives his 400 metres gold medal. Above: That's my new world record for the 200 metres, folks

Michael Johnson of the USA is just a sprinter. One who is not only in a class of his own, but a whole school. At Atlanta, Johnson broke new ground by winning both the 400 metres and 200 metres track events. No one had done it before.

No one thought it possible – except Johnson. The double was always on his mind, even before,

as expected, he bagged the 400 metres. Some clung to the hope that the 400 heats and final might have tired Johnson a little for the 200, the event in which he had broken a 17-year-old world record just a month before.

He was not tired. He didn't just win the 200 – he owned it. So stunning was his run that he smashed that month-old world record by one-third of a second, and managed to drag Frankie Fredreicks and Ato Boldon under the pre-Johnson world record mark.

The fastest man on earth? He has yet to compete in the 100 metres. But he indicated at Atlanta that he could well add that to his repertoire as well.

Christie storms out
Atlanta 1996

L inford Christie, shirtless, walked down the 100 metres track and waved to the crowd. It was a farewell from the reigning Olympic champion, but not a fond one. Christie had not been given the chance to defend his 1992 title – or rather he had but had blown it without breaking sweat.

He was ignominiously thrown out of the 100 metres final for causing two false starts. He was even shown the red card for protesting to officials.

The problem? In a generally twitchy start to a tension-filled final, Christie, with one false start already against him, was deemed to have raised a shoulder a fraction too early. A mere 14 hundredths of a second too early, according to the freeze-framed image.

By such narrow margins are fates decided. Not the greatest way to say goodbye to a distinguished champion.

"I lost my Olympic title, but I can't say I was beaten because I wasn't in the race. The crowd knew they'd been robbed of a race that would have been much better if I had been in it."
Linford Christie

Despair: Linford Christie is shown the red card and trudges out of the Atlanta Olympics

'La Gazelle' with a soupçon of ooh-la-la

Atlanta 1996

While Michael Johnson took the bulk of the plaudits for his 200/400 double gold at Atlanta, fans of Guadeloupe-born French runner Marie-Jose Perec would like to point out that their girl beat Johnson to the double by a matter of minutes.

Perec, nicknamed La Gazelle, sprinted past Merlene Ottey to take the women's 200 gold to add to the 400 she had already won, before Johnson had lined up for the start of his climactic race.

In the 400 metres four days earlier, Perec, the defending

"I'm like Michael Jordan in my own country. I can't walk in the street without being bothered. Now people are going to go crazy, I think."

Marie-Jose Perec

Olympic champion, had set a new Olympic record in claiming the gold once more. For the 200 she lined up against one of her sprinting idols, Ottey, who was her usual explosive self out of the blocks. But the long-striding Perec always had her in her sights. And with 15 metres between Ottey and that first elusive gold medal in the Olympics, Perec glided past and into the history books. Happy for herself, but at the same time sad for Ottey.

Shattered idol: Marie-Jose Perec wins the 200 metres from Merlene Ottey

95

Perec *factfile*

Born: 9.5.1968, Basse-Terre, Guadeloupe

Country: France

Olympic record: 1992: 400m gold
1996: 200m gold, 400m gold

Smith *factfile*

Born: 1970
Country: Ireland
Winner of three golds in Atlanta, and also a bronze in the 200m butterfly event. Banned in 1998 for four years after irregularities in a drug test.

96

The Irish torpedo

Atlanta 1996

Michelle Smith was the big story of the 1996 Games. On the plus side she was making headlines, particularly back home in Ireland, for superb performances in the pool. She won three gold medals – in the 400 metres medley, the 400 metres freestyle and the 200 metres individual medley. All that from a girl whose country of birth didn't even have a 50-metre pool.

On the downside was the whispering, and then accusations from fellow competitors, particularly the Americans, that Smith's amazing improvement – she reduced

"I just have to laugh at it. Every time I'm tested I come up negative, and I have been tested again and again and again. For every time someone on the US team is tested, I'm tested five times."

Michelle Smith, who was later banned after a drugs test

her personal best in the 400 metres freestyle by 19 seconds in 15 months – must be due to illegal aid in the form of performance-

Smith powering through the 400 metres freestyle and left, celebrating victory in the 400 individual medley

enhancing drugs. Each time she won a medal the questions intensified. Smith pointed out that she hadn't failed a drugs test. She attributed her improvements to a new training programme devised by her husband. The fact is that the allegations were unsubstantiated – and Michelle Smith won three gold medals. But her accusers will have taken satisfaction in 1998 when Smith was banned for four years because of irregularities in a drugs test.

97

"He's a great athlete; gosh, he's a great athlete. I'm 29 and my body feels like it's 60. Carl's 35 and he's still doing this. Someday I hope my kids ask me 'Dad, did you ever beat Carl Lewis?' That's his legacy."

Joe Greene – long jump bronze medallist 1996

Lewis makes it nine!
Atlanta 1996

O n the same night that Michael Johnson sprinted to the first half of what would be a historic running double, Carl Lewis made history of his own. The man who had been a constant of the US Olympic team since he burst on to the scene in 1984, registered a long jump of 27ft ten-and-three-quarter inches. It was his longest jump at a non-altitude event since the Barcelona Olympics four years earlier. As in Barcelona, he won gold. By winning, Lewis matched American discus thrower Al Oerter, who won four consecutive Olympic gold medals in his event from 1956 to 1968. Lewis launched himself to four consecutive golds in the long-jump pit – but he has won five other Olympic golds as well.

It had been a hard journey for Lewis to even compete for his ninth and final gold medal. He had missed a lot of competition in the previous three years because of injury or illness. But a new diet, new training regime and much dedication returned him to fitness.

His form wasn't as sublime as in previous Games, and it was the first time since 1976 that the long-jump gold medallist had not cleared 28 feet.

But with US rival Mike Powell tearing his hamstring (and still attempting one more forlorn effort to beat Lewis), less than 28 feet was still good enough – though waiting to see if anyone would beat the mark he set on only his third jump was tense, and probably added to his 35 years.

But at least he knew he wouldn't have to go through the waiting again. Carl Lewis – the King of track and field – retired on top.

Lewis *factfile*

Born: 1961 **Country:** USA
Olympic record: 1984: matched Jesse Owens' feat of winning gold in 100m, 200m, 4x100m and long jump. 1988: won gold in 100m and long jump, silver medal in 200m. 1992: long jump gold and 4x100m gold in world record time. 1996: long jump gold – the second Olympian ever to win four in a row in the same event. Tied with Mark Spitz at the head of the official medal tally for the Games with nine golds.

The final leap: Lewis goes for gold for the last time

Merlene Ottey's long sprint career in the Olympics was never rewarded with gold. In total, the Jamaican won seven medals in five Olympics: five bronze plus the two silver medals at Atlanta.

Merlene Ottey (centre) in her final chance for gold, loses out to Gail Devers (right) in the 100 metres

Ottey denied again
Atlanta 1996

From 1980 to 1996, Merlene Ottey ran her heart out for Jamaica in the 100 metres, 200 metres and 4x100 metres. But despite being recognised as one of the best sprinters in the world, she never won the Olympic gold medal that she coveted so much.

The Atlanta Games were to be her last chance and the omens, again, were not good. Marie-Jose Perec had denied her gold in the 200 metres when Ottey was overhauled in the final 10 metres of the race.

In the 100 metres she really thought she had a chance. In one of the closest finishes in Olympic sprint history, Ottey crossed the line in exactly the same time as defending champion Gail Devers – 10.94 seconds.

The decision went to the American by the margin of just five thousandths of a second – more disappointment for the 30-year-old Ottey, who had to settle for her second silver medal of the 1996 Games.

Her last thread of hope

"If it's the head, Gail won, if it's the torso, I won."
Merlene Ottey
on the closeness of the finish

came from the protest by the Jamaican delegation, who claimed that the photo-finish had been misinterpreted. But the result stood and Ottey didn't get that elusive gold.

Ottey *factfile*

Born: 10.5.1966
Country: Jamaica
Olympic record: 1980: 200m silver, 4x100m relay sixth
1984: 100m bronze, 200m bronze
1988: 200m fourth
1992: 200m bronze, 100m fifth
1996: 100m silver, 200m silver, 4x100m relay bronze

98

Kerri leads the Magnificent Seven
Atlanta 1996

99

The Russians were favourites for the women's gymnastics gold at Atlanta – yet it was the home team who found themselves in the lead as they came to the final apparatus, the vault. Dominique Moceanu, with the opportunity to pull off a surprise victory, slipped on both her vaults. So the Americans' final chance lay with Kerri Strug from Tucson, Arizona, who had been part of the bronze medal-winning team at Barcelona four years earlier.

Then, Kerri had been the youngest US athlete. Now, having turned 18, she already considered herself over the hill! Strug had been injured since Barcelona, but had bounced back to win the vault in the Olympic trials and so would jump last.

Kerri's first vault was a disaster. As she landed, she slipped and fell, injuring her leg. As she limped off the mat, it looked as if America's chance had limped off with her.

But after having her leg bandaged, Kerri insisted she was OK, and wanted to give her second vault a try. Bandage flapping, she ran in as fast as she could and hit the vault. As her feet thumped on the floor, it was obvious she was in great pain. But, with teeth gritted, she held her position long enough to be given a mark of 9.712 and clinch Olympic gold for the US for the first time.

Kerri and her teammates – Amanda Borden, Amy Chow, Dominique Dawes, Shannon Miller, Dominique Moceanu and Jaycie Phelps – have since become known as the Magnificent Seven. But the heroine of the hour, who had to be carried to the podium to collect her medal, was that gritty fighter Kerri Strug.

Coach Bela Karolyi carries Kerri Strug to the winner's rostrum

Strug *factfile*

Name: Kerri Strug
Born: June 12, 1977
Olympic record: 1996: gold team gymnastics gold. Youngest American athlete at the 1992 Barcelona Olympics.

When the final whistle blew in the Olympic football final, it signalled the arrival of a new power on the world soccer scene – Nigeria.

In the space of two games, the semi-final and then the final, the Nigerian Eagles – largely the country's under-23 squad sent to Atlanta to gain international experience – beat two of the world's best and showed that African countries could play the game well.

The semi-final against mighty Brazil was a classic, played out in front of 78,000 fans. The Brazilians, full of attacking flair as ever, took

---

Top scorer in the Olympic football event was Sophus Nielsen of Denmark who, in the 1908 Games, netted 11 times as his country took the silver medal.

---

a stranglehold on the game and led 3-1 after 37 minutes. When the Nigerians missed a penalty in the 63rd minute, it seemed as if the final would be snatched away. But Victor Ikpeba

The Eagles have landed
Atlanta 1996

made it 3-2 in the 77th minutes, and then Nwankwo Kanu, with little time left, thundered home the equaliser to force extra time.

It was golden-goal extra time, too. Next goal wins. And it was Kanu, later of Arsenal, who made Nigerian history by steering home the winner. In the final, the excite-

ment continued. Argentina were beaten 3-2 but the Nigerian winning goal came only in the dying minutes.

Cue final whistle. Cue the celebrations all across Africa.

Above: Kanu is carried off in triumph as Nigeria celebrate a historic victory. Left: Flowers and medals for the Olympic champions

Summer Games

Olympiad	Year	Venue	Men	Women	Total	Nations
I	1896	Athens	c.200	0	c.200	14
II	1900	Paris	1,206	19	1,225	26
III	1904	St Louis	681	6	687	13
IV	1908	London	1,999	36	2,035	22
V	1912	Stockholm	2,490	57	2,547	28
VI	1916	Berlin	Cancelled			
VII	1920	Antwerp	2,591	77	2,668	29
VIII	1924	Paris	2,956	136	3,092	44
IX	1928	Amsterdam	2,724	290	3,014	46
X	1932	Los Angeles	1,281	127	1,408	37
XI	1936	Berlin	3,758	328	4,066	49
XII	1940	Helsinki	Cancelled			
XIII	1944	London	Cancelled			
XIV	1948	London	3,714	385	4,099	59
XV	1952	Helsinki	4,407	518	4,925	69
XVI	1956	Melbourne	2,813	371	3,184	67
	1956	Stockholm*	145	13	158	29
XVII	1960	Rome	4,736	610	5,346	83
XVIII	1964	Tokyo	4,457	683	5,140	93
XIX	1968	Mexico City	4,749	781	5,530	112
XX	1972	Munich	6,065	1,058	7,123	121
XXI	1976	Montreal	4,781	1,247	6,028	92
XXII	1980	Moscow	4,043	1,124	5,217	80
XXIII	1984	Los Angeles	5,230	1,567	6,797	140
XXIV	1988	Seoul	6,279	2,186	8,465	159
XXV	1992	Barcelona	6,657	2,707	9,364	169
XXVI	1996	Atlanta	6,797	3,513	10,310	197

* Equestrian events in 1956 were held in Stockholm due to Australia's quarantine laws

Left: A torch-bearer epitomises the Aryan ideal at Berlin in 1936 – the year in which the tradition of carrying the torch from Olympia to the Olympic Games was initiated – and speedskating at Albertville in 1992

Winter Games

Olympiad	Year	Venue	Men	Women	Total	Nations
I	1924	Chamonix	245	13	258	16
II	1928	St Moritz	438	26	464	25
III	1932	Lake Placid	231	21	252	17
IV	1936	Garmisch-Partenkirchen	588	80	668	28
V	1948	St Moritz	529	77	606	28
VI	1952	Oslo	585	109	694	30
VII	1956	Cortina d'Ampezzo	688	132	820	32
VIII	1960	Squaw Valley	522	143	665	30
IX	1964	Innsbruck	891	200	1,091	36
X	1968	Grenoble	947	211	1,158	37
XI	1972	Sapporo	800	206	1,006	35
XII	1976	Innsbruck	892	231	1,123	37
XIII	1980	Lake Placid	839	233	1,072	37
XIV	1984	Sarajevo	1,000	274	1,274	49
XV	1988	Calgary	1,110	313	1,423	57
XVI	1992	Albertville	1,313	488	1,801	64
XVII	1994	Lillehammer	1,217	520	1,737	67
XVIII	1998	Nagano	1,570	607	2,177	72

Left: The Olympic rings – a symbol adopted in 1920 – decorate the ice at Albertville, 1992. Right: A poster for the Stockholm equestrian event; a British stamp celebrating the 1948 Games; and spectators at Lillehammer, 1994

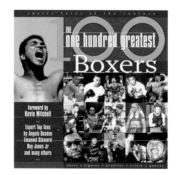

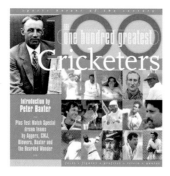

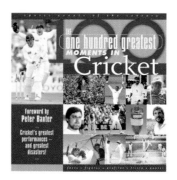

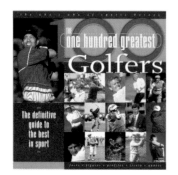

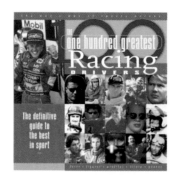

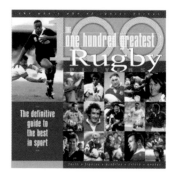